Workbook 16

Communication

Manage Information
Certificate
S/NVQ Level 4

Institute of Management Open Learning Programme

Series editor: Gareth Lewis
Author: Cathy Lake

chartered

management

institute

Pergamon
Flexible
Learning

Pergamon Flexible Learning
An imprint of Elsevier Science
Linacre House, Jordan Hill, Oxford OX2 8DP
200 Wheeler Road, Burlington, MA 01803

First published 1997
Reprinted 1998, 1999, 2000, 2001, 2002, 2003

British Library Cataloguing in Publication Data
A catalogue record for this book is available from the British Library

ISBN 0 7506 3674 2

For information on all Butterworth-Heinemann publications
visit our website at www.bh.com

Printed and bound in Great Britain

FOR EVERY TITLE THAT WE PUBLISH, BUTTERWORTH-HEINEMANN
WILL PAY FOR BTCV TO PLANT AND CARE FOR A TREE.

Contents

Series overview

The Institute of Management Open Learning Programme is a series of workbooks prepared by the Institute of Management and Pergamon Open Learning for managers seeking to develop themselves.

Comprising seventeen open learning workbooks, the programme covers the best of modern management theory and practice, and each workbook provides a range of frameworks and techniques to improve your effectiveness as a manager, thus helping you acquire the knowledge and skill to make you fully competent in your role.

Each workbook is written by an experienced management writer and covers an important management topic or theme. The activities both reinforce learning and help to relate the generic ideas to your individual work context. While coverage of each topic is fully comprehensive, additional reading suggestions and reference sources are given for those who wish to study to a greater depth.

Designed to be practical, stimulating and challenging, the aim of the workbooks is to improve performance at work by benefiting you and your organization. This practical focus is at the heart of the competence based approach that has been adopted by the programme.

The structure of the programme

The design and overall structure of the programme has two main organizing principles, both of which are closely linked to the national standards for management developed by the MCI (Management Charter Initiative).

First, the workbooks are grouped according to the key roles of management.

- Underpinning the management standards are a series of **personal competences** which describe the personal skills required by all managers, which are essential to skill in all the main functional or key role areas.
- **Manage Activities** describes the principles of managing processes and activities, with service to the customer as an essential part of this.
- **Manage Resources** describes the acquisition, control and monitoring of financial and other resources.
- **Manage People** looks at the key skills involved in leadership, developing one's staff and managing their performance.

■ **Manage Information** discusses the acquisition, storage and use of
   information for communication, problem solving and decision making.

In addition, there are three specialized key roles: **Manage Quality,
Manage Projects** and **Manage Energy**. The workbooks cover the first two
of these. Unlike the four primary key roles above, these are not compulsory
for certificate, diploma or S/NVQ requirements, but provide options for the
latter.

Together, these key roles provide a comprehensive description of the
fundamental principles of management as it applies in any organization –
commercial, maintained sector or not-for-profit.

Second, the programme is organized according to **levels of management**, seniority and responsibility.

Level 4 represents first line management. In accredited programmes
this is equivalent to S/NVQ Level 4, Certificate in Management or CMS.
Level 5 is equivalent to middle/senior management and is accredited at
S/NVQ Level 5, Diploma in Management or DMS. There are two S/NVQs at
Level 5: Operational Management and Strategic Management. The operations
role is focussed internally within an organization on the maintenance of systems and standards of output, whilst the strategic role is focussed on the
whole organization, including the external operating environment, and looks
at setting directions.

Together, the workbooks cover all the background knowledge you
need to have for all units of competence in the MCI standards at Level 4 and
Level 5 (apart from the specialized units in the key role Manage Energy). They
also provide skills development and opportunities for portfolio building.

For a comprehensive list of workbooks, see page ix. For a comprehensive list of links with the standards, see the *User Guide*.

How to use the programme

The programme is deliberately designed to be flexible and can be used
in a variety of ways:

■ to update on important management topics and themes, or develop individual
   skills: as the workbooks are grouped according to themes, it should be easy for
   you to pick out one that suits your needs

■ as part of generic management development programmes: you can choose the
   modules that fit the themes of the programme

■ as part of, and in support of, accredited competence-based programmes.

For N/SVQs at both Levels 4 and 5, there are options in the combinations of units that make up the various awards. By using the map provided in the *User Guide*, individuals will be able to select the workbooks appropriate to their specific needs, and their chosen accreditation options. Some of the activities will help you provide evidence for your portfolio; where we think this is the case, we give the relevant reference to the standards.

For Certificate or CMS, Diploma or DMS, individuals should choose modules that not only meet their individual needs but also satisfy the requirements of the delivering body and the awarding body.

You may need help and guidance in these choices, and the *User Guide* sets out the options and advice in much more detail. A fuller description of the potential uses of this material in evidence gathering and portfolio building can also be found in the *User Guide*, as can a detailed description of the contents of each workbook.

Workbooks in the Institute of Management Open Learning Programme

Personal Competences (Levels 4 and 5)

1 *The Influential Manager**
2 *Managing Yourself**

Manage Activities (Level 4)

3 *Understanding Business Process Management*
4 *Customer Focus*

Manage Activities (Level 5)

5 *Getting TQM to Work*
6 *Leading from the Front*
7 *Improving Your Organization's Success*

Manage Resources (Level 4)

8 *Project Management*
9 *Budgeting and Financial Control*

Manage Resources (Level 5)

10 *Effective Financial and Resource Management*

Manage People (Level 4)

1 *The Influential Manager*
2 *Managing Yourself*
11 *Getting the Right People to do the Right Job*
12 *Developing Yourself and Your Staff*
13 *Building a High Performance Team*

Manage People (Level 5)

14 *The New Model Leader*

Manage Information (Level 4)

15 *Making Rational Decisions*
16 *Communication*

Manage Information (Level 5)

17 *Successful Information Management*

Manage Quality (Level 4)

3 *Understanding Business Process Management**
4 *Customer Focus**

Manage Quality (Level 5)

5 *Getting TQM to Work**

Manage Projects (Level 4)

8 *Project Management**

Manage Projects (Level 5)

8 *Project Management**

Support Materials

18 *User Guide*
19 *Mentor Guide*

An asterisk indicates that a particular workbook also contains material suitable for a particular key role or personal competence.

Links to qualifications

S/NVQ programmes

This workbook can help candidates to achieve credit and develop skills in the key role of managing people and covers the following units and elements:

D2 Facilitate meetings
D2.1 Lead meetings
D2.2 Make contributions to meetings
D3 Chair and participate in meetings
D3.1 Chair meetings
D3.2 Participate in meetings
D4.4 Advise and inform others

Certificate and Diploma programmes

This workbook, together with the other Level 4 workbook on managing information (15 – *Making Rational Decisions*), covers all of the knowledge required in the key role Manage Information for Certificate in Management and CMS programmes.

Links to other workbooks

The other workbook in the key role Manage Information at Level 4 is:.

15 *Making Rational Decisions*

The Level 5 module in this key role is:

17 *Successful Information Management*

The theme of communication is also dealt with in Workbook 2, *Managing Yourself*.

Introduction

You already know a lot about communication. You have, after all, been communicating all your life. So why is it so important for managers to study communication skills?

First, the fact that you are communicating with other people all the time means that the process has probably become largely automatic. For most people, there are so many other aspects of their working lives which require serious thought that they normally concentrate on the **content** of what they read, hear, write and say – not on the way the message gets across. It is worth taking a long, hard look at any process that has become automatic, to check that it really is doing the job it is meant to do – and doing it in the most effective way.

We learn our basic communication skills as children, before we are capable of abstract or theoretical thought. As adults, we refine these skills, but may actually still be following old patterns and habits which have long outlived their purpose. There are some general principles of communication which you won't have been taught when you were learning to speak and write, but which you can now use to improve your performance.

Another important reason for looking at how you communicate is that these skills are central to your managerial role. In essence, the job of a manager is to organize other people in order to translate ideas into reality. This involves receiving and passing on information, receiving and giving instructions – and changing attitudes. These are all communications tasks. The more effectively you can communicate, the more effective a manager you can be.

Finally, there are some specialized forms of communication, such as chairing a meeting or giving a presentation, which you may not have had much experience of before you became a manager. There are conventions and techniques to be learned here – and you will have an opportunity to explore these areas later in the book. In this first section, we will lay the foundations by discussing some general concepts which can be applied to any form of communication.

Objectives

By the end of this workbook you should be able to:

- Deliver information in writing, orally and via electronic media
- Communicate effectively through appropriate media
- Contribute to meetings and group discussions
- Influence and manage colleagues through discussion and persuasion

Section 1   The basics of communication

Are you receiving me?

Sometimes even the best communicators are thrown off their stride. Picture this:

A radio news presenter is in the middle of a broadcast. Suddenly, something goes wrong with the system connecting his headset to the outside world. He cannot hear the answers of the politician he has on the line and is obliged to abandon the interview. Worse still, he cannot hear the instructions of his producer in his ear. Without this reassurance, he no longer knows whether his own voice is being heard by listeners. This professional broadcaster, who is normally in total control of his medium, is reduced to a state of near panic:

'Er ... I'm sorry ... but I can't ... I can't continue with that interview ... Um ... we seem to have a tech ... a technical problem ... I'm sorry, but I can't ... I can't communicate ... I can't communicate with anyone ...'

He is only able to continue with the programme when the producer convinces him, by hand signals through the glass, that his voice is actually being broadcast live to the nation.

You are unlikely to experience a communications nightmare of quite these proportions, but you have almost certainly had the disconcerting experience of getting no response from the person you are trying to speak to. Parents know this feeling well. You may have had the frustration of leaving messages on an answerphone and not being phoned back, or perhaps you know what it feels like when someone you are trying to impress appears not to have noticed your existence.

ACTIVITY 1

Think of an occasion when you were trying to communicate with someone and received no indication from them that your message was getting through.

1   What was the incident?

2   What effect did this lack of response have on you?

FEEDBACK

One of the following words probably sums up how you felt in this situation:

■   angry
■   powerless
■   bewildered
■   embarrassed
■   puzzled

It is extraordinarily hard to communicate if we get no feedback. In fact, real communication is impossible in these circumstances.

Let's look at the elements which are necessary for communication to take place. First, there must be someone who is trying to communicate:

SENDER

There must also be something which the sender is trying to communicate:

SENDER ⇒ MESSAGE ⇒

This message can be a piece of information, an idea, a request, or even a sensation. It is also necessary for the message to be directed at someone:

SENDER   ⇒ MESSAGE ⇒   RECEIVER

Finally, for real communication to be established, the sender must get some feedback from the receiver, which indicates that the message has arrived.

SENDER   ⇒ MESSAGE ⇒   RECEIVER
          ⇐ FEEDBACK ⇐

It is not necessary for the receiver to **agree** with the message for communication to have taken place. Feedback can often be negative. All that is necessary is that the sender receives an acknowledgement that the message has been received.

As human beings, we have a very strong need to know that we are in communication with other individuals. You can see how powerful this need is if you consider the moments in films which audiences find the most moving. Film makers can always bring a lump to our throats with scenes like these:

- a coma victim hears a familiar voice and opens his eyes
- at the last moment before a boat sinks, a helicopter responding to a Mayday call comes over the horizon
- a prisoner alone in a cell taps on the pipework and hears an answering knock from another inmate of the jail

You can probably think of many scenes like these, when a character with whom we identify finds that his or her message has been received. They are powerful moments. They remind us that the most crucial aspect of communication is that the person who initiates a message knows that it has been received.

In ordinary life, the feedback we receive can take many forms:

Manager: After I've finished a presentation, it's great if someone comes up and says 'Thanks, that was really interesting, I enjoyed that'.

Teacher: At the start of a lesson, I stand up and clap my hands. When the noise in the classroom dies down, I know I've got the children's attention.

Nurse: I know if I've said the right things to patients on the ward by the way they look at me.

Publicity manager: I know we've produced an excellent brochure if 10% of the people we send it to fill in the coupon for more details.

The more concerned you are about how your message was received, or whether it was received at all, the more important feedback becomes to you.

ACTIVITY 2

Think of a situation in which it was important to you to know that your message had been received. What type of feedback did you need?

Situation:

Feedback

FEEDBACK

Your situation and the feedback you required may have had something in common with these answers:

I had to get a set of accounts to the Inland Revenue by a particular date. I sent the letter by registered post, so that I got a signature at the other end to confirm it had arrived.

I had to brief my assistant about what to do with some very important visitors who she would have to look after while I was in a meeting. It was essential that everything went perfectly, so I got her to draw up a schedule for the visit and show it to me.

In some types of communication, all the sender needs is an acknowledgement that the message has been received. In other situations, messages have to be sent and received in both directions. In these circumstances, both parties may need reassurance that their message has got across.

ACTIVITY 3

In the following extract from a telephone conversation, underline the lines of dialogue where either of the speakers is making sure that their message has been received and understood.

A: Can you send me a catalogue please?

B: Are you private or business?

A: Um ... I wanted a catalogue of your office furniture.

B: Is it for a company?

A: No, it's for my own use at home.

B: Then it'll be private. Can I have your name, please?

A: Catherine Scott.

B: Is that with a C or a K?

C: With a C. And Scott is spelt with two Ts.

FEEDBACK

You should have underlined these lines:

A: Um ... I wanted a catalogue about your office furniture.

(A is not sure that B has understood her request, so she repeats and amplifies it.)

B: Is it for a company?

(B rephrases her question, because A has not answered it.)

C: With a C. And Scott is spelt with two Ts.

(A checks that B is spelling her surname correctly.)

When you are communicating with someone else, whether you are talking face-to-face, exchanging letters or e-mails, or speaking on the telephone, you should always:

- give the other person the reassurance they need that you have understood their message
- make it absolutely clear what feedback you require from them

ANTICIPATING THE RESPONSE

Successful communicators know the response they are trying to achieve, and do everything they can to get it. Before they begin communicating, they think about how their message will be received and the likely reaction it will provoke. However, not everyone is a successful communicator.

ACTIVITY 4

Think of colleagues whom you would describe as poor communicators in the following types of situation:

■ meetings

■ writing

■ face-to-face conversations

What are they doing wrong? And what effect do these mistakes have on you?

I communicating in meetings

■ mistake

■ effect

2 communicating in writing

■ mistake

■ effect

3 communicating face-to-face

- mistake

- effect

Compare your answers with these:

1 communicating in meetings

'Once A opens his mouth, he won't stop talking. I get bored and frustrated.'
'B always turns a discussion into a personal argument. It's embarrassing.'

2 communicating in writing

'C always uses such technical language in her reports that they go straight over my head. I find them so difficult that I don't bother reading them.'
'D never answers a letter until he's had it on his desk for at least a week. It's irritating and insulting, as though his time is worth much more than anyone else's.'

3 communicating face-to-face

'E speaks so quickly that I can't remember half of what he asks me do. It intimidates me.'
'F has a funny way of looking at you when you're talking, as though she doesn't believe a word of what you're telling her. I find it very disconcerting and do my best to avoid talking to her.'

Whatever examples you came up with yourself, it's likely that they had something to do with the fact that poor communicators rarely think about the effect their message (or the way they put it across) will have.

Sometimes you are not sure about the response your piece of communication will get. If this response is important, it is important to test your communication before you present it to its real audience. You should probably show drafts of difficult letters to colleagues before sending them off, and rehearse a presentation or speech in front of people who will give you constructive criticism. Many organizations use focus groups to judge how new activities will be received by a wider audience.

If you can **anticipate** the response your message will get, you can put yourself in a position where you can stay in control of the exchange. Read this account from a departmental manager:

CASE STUDY

Recently, a relatively junior member of my staff applied for the post of deputy departmental manager. He wasn't ready for promotion yet, but I believed he would certainly be a candidate for promotion in the future. It was a slightly difficult situation, because I knew he was not a particularly confident person and he would be upset when he heard that he wasn't even on the short list. I could have sent him a letter, and not said anything in the office to him at all, but I didn't think this would be fair.

What I did was this. On the day when the letters asking people for interview went out, I called him into my office at the end of the afternoon. I didn't warn him beforehand, because this would have put him off his work. When the door was shut and he was sitting down, I told him straightaway that he hadn't made the interview list for this job because I felt that he was not yet ready for it, and that a letter was going out to him with this information. I said this as clearly as possible, so there was no possibility of misunderstanding. I didn't explain further. If we'd got into a discussion, he might have said something he regretted later, because he was upset by the news. I told him I was glad that he'd made the application, because it showed that he was thinking seriously about his career with the company. I told him that I believed that he did have a good future ahead of him with us, when he had gained more experience. Then I handed him a brochure describing the training courses available to people on his grade and asked him to study it that evening and think about the direction he would like to take. I asked him to come back and see me next week, when we would discuss possibilities and draw up a development plan for him. Then I thanked him for coming in and stood up and opened the door. And off he went.

ACTIVITY 5

Make a list of things that the departmental manager did because she anticipated the reactions of the unsuccessful applicant.

FEEDBACK

You should have picked up most of these points:

- She spoke to him personally
- She timed the meeting so that he would not have to talk to colleagues when he was upset
- She did not forewarn him, so he would not have to worry about the meeting beforehand
- She spoke to him in private, to avoid embarrassment
- She explained the situation simply, so he would not have to ask for clarification
- She avoided a discussion in which he might have said something he regretted later
- She gave him some positive feedback
- She gave him something to look forward to
- She concluded the exchange quickly

What the departmental manager did was to think about how her message was going to be received and plan her communication accordingly.

Planning your communication

Nobody in their right mind stands up to give a presentation without preparing what they are going to say. Most people spend many hours in planning and drafting a public piece of communication like this. Yet the same people are often quite capable of picking up the phone or sending a quick memo without giving any consideration to what they are saying or how they should say it – and then being surprised when they don't get the reaction they expect.

Planning pays off when you are making any type of communication, no matter how trivial it seems. Often, this simply involves pausing for a moment and reminding yourself of a few basic issues:

■ the purpose of your communication
■ your audience
■ the content of what you are saying
■ the timing of your communication
■ your means of communication

We will now look at these issues in some more detail.

THE PURPOSE OF YOUR COMMUNICATION

When you are at work, the most usual reasons to communicate with other people are:

■ to give information
■ to give instructions
■ to obtain information
■ to take instructions
■ to persuade someone to do something

ACTIVITY 6

1   Think about the last six times you communicated with anyone at work. Include times when you spoke face-to-face, on the telephone, in writing or in any other way. Tick the boxes to show why you were communicating each time.

Your communication	Giving information	Giving instructions	Taking instructions	Getting information	Persuading
1	❏	❏	❏	❏	❏
2	❏	❏	❏	❏	❏
3	❏	❏	❏	❏	❏
4	❏	❏	❏	❏	❏
5	❏	❏	❏	❏	❏
6	❏	❏	❏	❏	❏

2   Generally, what is your most frequent reason for communicating with other people when you are at work?

FEEDBACK

Your answers to this activity will obviously reflect the nature of your work. Most managers are somewhere in the middle of a chain of command and have to do all of these things at some time or other.

If you are clear about your purpose when you are communicating, you have a greater chance of achieving your aim. If you are not clear, misunderstandings can arise:

Secretary: Just before she went into a meeting, my boss said 'I'm expecting that company in the Netherlands to ring this morning'. I thought she was just warning me so I'd have the papers ready. But what she actually meant was that she wanted me to get her out of the meeting to take the call.

The secretary thought that her boss was giving her information, whereas she was really trying to give her instructions.

Manager: The Training Department put on a series of evening seminars about time management. I told three of my staff to attend, but since it was a voluntary course, they refused.

This manager gave instructions when he should have been persuading.

The more precise you can be about your objectives for a piece of communication, the better. Most people have experienced the irritation of ending a phone call or posting a letter and then realizing they have forgotten to ask for an essential piece of information or provide an important fact. You can avoid this by clarifying your purpose in advance.

ACTIVITY 7	D4.4

Use the following checklist to plan a piece of communication you have to make in the near future.

1   I need to communicate with _____

about

_____

2   What do I want to happen as a result of this communication?
    a   in the short term

_____

_____

b in the long term?

_____

_____

_____

3 What has to be communicated to make this possible?

_____

_____

_____

4 What has to be communicated to make this more likely to happen?

_____

_____

_____

5 How will I check that the message has been received?

_____

_____

_____

FEEDBACK

It is important to distinguish between what you hope will happen as a result of a communication in the long and the short term. For example, the purpose of your communication might be to ask a junior member of staff to print a document for you. Your short-term objective is to get the document printed, but your long-term objective might be to enable this individual to operate the printer without supervision. This could affect the amount of information you give about the printer.

This leads us on to the next issue to think about when planning a communication.

THE CONTENT OF YOUR COMMUNICATION

The actual content of what you say or write should, to a large extent, be determined by your purpose. There are also some other general rules which are useful to remember.

In any situation, there are some things which:

- you absolutely must say
- it would be useful to add
- you would like to say if you have the opportunity

ACTIVITY 8

On the way to a meeting at which you are going to raise a difficult question about the consequences to your department of lack of funding, you share a lift with a colleague whom you haven't seen for some time. You have 30 seconds to talk.

Prioritize the following information by writing the following letters in the boxes:

A   essential information

B   useful information

C   extra information

I   ☐   You have heard that the managing director has accepted your colleague's advice about a new training scheme and will make an announcement about it at the meeting.

2 ☐ You met a mutual friend at a social occasion at the weekend.

3 ☐ You would appreciate his support when you bring up the issue of funding.

FEEDBACK

I   may be useful information, but it is not crucial to your purposes, so it should be classified B.

2   is not important in this context, so it should be classified as C.

3   is the only essential piece of information that you need to get across in the time available, so this should be classified as A.

The best approach in this situation would be to start by asking for support in the meeting, and, if you have time, tell your colleague that his advice on the training scheme has been taken. Don't mention meeting the mutual friend, or you will spend the whole lift journey discussing him and not have time to get the essential information across.

When you have a very limited time available to communicate, it is relatively easy to prioritize what you have to say. You should exercise similar discipline whenever you communicate. Although an opportunity for communication may appear open-ended, it probably isn't.

It is important to remember:

- the time the person on the receiving end has available – busy people do not want to read interminable reports or rambling memos, or listen to unnecessary explanations
- the interest the other person has in the subject – the more relevant your subject is to their own needs and concerns, the more they will want to know
- the attention span of your audience – even if what you are communicating is absolutely fascinating, nobody can keep their attention up indefinitely without a break

If 90% of what you say is unnecessary or irrelevant, your audience may miss the crucial 10%. So, keep it short and simple.

Remember that your listeners or readers will not maintain the same level of concentration all the way through a long communication. You have the best chance of getting over important points at the beginning and the end of a conversation. Newspapers put the big news on the front page and catalogue compilers put new products in the opening pages. In a report, you summarize the essential findings in an executive summary at the beginning.

> 1 Think about the attention span of your audience
> 2 Prioritize what you want to say
> 3 Arrange the contents of your communication so that the most important points gain maximum impact

THINKING ABOUT YOUR AUDIENCE

You must also adapt your communication to the needs of your audience. Think about:

- what they know already
- what they need to know
- what they want to know
- any preconceptions they bring to the situation
- what they are capable of understanding

ACTIVITY 9

Imagine that there has been a rumour going round your organization that closure is imminent. This is not true, but every department is going to have to make a 15% budget cut in the next year. You call a meeting of the staff to explain the situation. Make some notes under the following headings. (You will find this activity works best if you imagine this scenario in the context of your real work situation.)

1   What they know already

2   What they need to know

3 What they want to know

4 Any preconceptions they bring to the situation

5 What they are capable of understanding

Your answers will reflect your knowledge of your own staff, but you should have borne the following points in mind:

1 What they know already.
Your staff will have heard the rumour. They will also have gained an impression of how successfully the organization has been operating recently. They may also have knowledge of outside events, such as a change in the market, which have some bearing on the situation.

2 What they need to know
They need to know that the rumour is unfounded, but that cuts will have to be made. They may need some proof that you are telling them the truth. Some of the information may be very sensitive and you may have to balance the need to maintain confidentiality against your staff's need to know about the situation.

3 What they want to know
They will be primarily interested in knowing how the cuts will affect them. Will there be redundancies? Will the workload change? Some individuals, such as those who would find it difficult to find another job or have particular financial difficulties, may want to speak to you privately to gain further reassurance.

4   Any preconceptions they bring to the situation
People may trust senior management to bring the organization through a difficult period – or they may have no confidence here. They may be hostile, frightened, or cynical.

5   What they are capable of understanding
It is a mistake to underestimate the intelligence of your audience. People generally know if they are being patronized or lied to. However, we all have different levels of education and areas of specialized knowledge. If your staff is not used to analysing financial information, you can't expect them to understand a complicated set of business ratios. On the other hand, everyone can see whether a line on a graph is going up or down. There may be some straightforward (and honest) way in which you can help them to appreciate the important facts. For example, you might decide to give the essential information fairly simply at the meeting and make further information available for people to take away and study afterwards.

When you work with people on a day-to-day basis, communication becomes easier. You acquire a shared vocabulary and can use technical terms with confidence. You also develop an awareness of the type of language that particular individuals appreciate. For example, you may speak very colloquially to one colleague, but much more formally to another. These adaptations happen naturally.

When you are communicating with people whom you don't know, you have to take much more care. Many people who pride themselves as good communicators try far too hard to adapt their message to their imagined audience. They may attempt to adopt the language patterns of the people they are addressing and even include appropriate cultural references. This usually has exactly the opposite effect to the one intended. It is extraordinarily difficult to use the language of a group to which you don't belong. You will probably embarrass your audience. There is also the danger that you will base your assumptions on false stereotypes and insult and alienate the people you are talking to.

I went to a talk given by a male manager about pension arrangements for clerical staff. Most of the audience were women in their 40s and 50s. One of the visual aids he used showed a cartoon of a couple on the deck of cruise ship, enjoying spending a lump sum. Honestly, what planet was he from? He had no idea of the financial realities which most people contend with these days.

Instead of trying to pretend that you are a member of a group you are addressing, bring your language to a neutral point where it is intelligible to anyone who doesn't share your own technical knowledge and cultural background.

GETTING THE TIMING RIGHT

The timing of your communication is also important. If you are replying to someone else, do it as quickly as possible. If people send an e-mail or a fax or leave a phone message, they usually expect an answer the same day. If they don't receive one, they may assume that you haven't got their message. The time which organizations take to answer letters varies enormously. Many commercial companies try to answer letters on the day they arrive. Some government offices, on the other hand, have a six-week backlog of correspondence. If you are going to delay more than a few days before answering, it is polite to send an acknowledgement to reassure the writer that you have received their letter.

When you are initiating a piece of communication, base your timing on your own needs and the needs of the receiver. Ask yourself:

- Do I have to get my message across by a certain date or time?
- How much of my receiver's time am I going to take up?
- What other demands does he/she have on his/her time?
- When is the best moment for him/her to give me the time I need?

So, if you want to present a lengthy report in advance of a meeting, consider how long it will take people to read it and allow them plenty of time to fit this into their schedule. If you know a telephone conversation is going to take several minutes, ask the person you ring whether this is a good moment for them to talk. Generally, the more consideration you show for other people's time, the more likely they are to give your communication the attention it deserves.

CHOOSING THE RIGHT CHANNEL

There are many different communication channels open to you. You can choose to get your message across:

- in a casual conversation
- in a pre-arranged conversation
- in a meeting (which can be large or small, formal or informal)
- in a presentation
- by phone
- by fax
- in a letter
- in a memo
- in a notice on a noticeboard
- by e-mail
- in a report
- in an internal newsletter
- in a brochure or other published literature

ACTIVITY 10

What channel (or channels) of communication would be appropriate for these messages?

1   Information about a social function at work

---

2   Confirmation that you have received an important order

---

3   An urgent request for detailed information from an overseas supplier

---

4   A proposal for a new project

---

5   An invitation to a job interview

---

6   A change to the procedure for processing expense claims

---

7   A request for suggestions about how to improve time-keeping

---

FEEDBACK

1 A notice on the noticeboard and a piece in an internal newsletter would be an appropriate way to tell everyone about a social function. When the date was close, you would probably want to remind people in casual conversations.

2 A telephone call, backed up by a letter giving written confirmation, would be appropriate here.

3 You could send the overseas supplier a fax or an e-mail.

4 A proposal for a new project would demand a written report, followed up by discussion at a meeting.

5 An invitation to a job interview is a confidential matter and should be done by letter.

6 People will need to keep a written record of a change to procedure. A memo would be appropriate.

7 A request for suggestions about how to improve time-keeping is something which requires feedback. It would be a suitable topic for a meeting.

This activity demonstrated some of the criteria which you should consider when choosing your means of communication:

■ the confidentiality of the information
■ the type of feedback you need
■ the urgency of the information
■ whether people need a written record – either for their own future reference or because this is necessary for legal reasons
■ how many people you need to communicate with at once
■ the importance of the information to the organization

Some people are more comfortable with one channel of communication than others and use it even when it is not particularly appropriate.

My manager sends me six or seven e-mails every day, even though he is sitting the other side of the office to me. Once he even sent me an e-mail asking if I wanted to buy a ticket in the office sweepstake. It's annoying, because I have to stop what I'm doing on the computer and check my mailbox, in case it's something urgent. Sometimes he should just get up and walk across the room to speak to me – or wait until we have a coffee break to have a word.

I explained the new safety procedure at the team meeting, but apparently this wasn't enough. I had to send everyone written details, too.

I telephoned my boss to tell him that we had a problem with a supplier. Later on, he denied that he'd ever received the call and blamed the deteriorating situation on me. I should have sent him a memo.

ACTIVITY 11

Which channels of communication do you feel most confident about using? Put a mark on each scale below to indicate how comfortable you feel with each of these methods.

	Very confident	Not at all confident
Casual conversation		
Small meeting		
Large meeting		
Presentation		
Phone		
Fax		
E-mail		
Letter		
Memo		
Report		
Notice		
Newsletter		

Now think of the last four communications you sent. What channel did you use? Why? Would another channel have been more appropriate?

I

Communication

_____

Channel

_____

Reason

Alternative channel next time?

2
Communication

Channel

Reason

Alternative channel next time?

3
Communication

Channel

Reason

Alternative channel next time?

4
Communication

Channel

_____

Reason

_____

Alternative channel next time?

_____

FEEDBACK

Most people have their own preferred channels of communication:

'I am much more confident talking to people on the phone than I am face-to-face.'

'If I can help it, I never have an important conversation on the phone. I need to see the face of the person I'm talking to, to see how they are reacting.'

'I hate writing letters because I'm worried my grammar will let me down.'

'I enjoy writing letters – they are a good way to build up a friendly working relationship with colleagues and suppliers.'

It is possible that your lack of confidence or experience with some channels of communication can sometimes lead you to pick an inappropriate method to get your message across. If this is true for you, highlight the areas of communication where you would like to develop your skills.

Once you have selected the appropriate channel, you need to use it effectively. You need to know its restrictions and conventions – and be able to exploit its possibilities to fulfil your own needs and the needs of your audience. This is what we will explore in the remainder of this book.

ACTIVITY 12

Conclude your work on this first section by considering the channel of communication in which you feel least confident of your skills. Use the following checklist to make yourself a plan for the next time you use this method of communication.

1   What feedback will you need, and how will you make sure you get it?
2   How will you take into account the needs of the person or people who will receive your communication?
3   How will you define your purpose?
4   How will you plan the content of your communication?
5   How will you plan the timing of your communication?
6   How will you assess the appropriateness of this method of communication?

Finally, make a list of questions you feel you would like to ask about this method of communication. Your questions could include points of information, such as:

■   How do I set out a report?
■   When is it OK to address someone by their first name in a letter?
■   How do I know if an e-mail has been received?

You may also have questions about particular skills, such as:

■   How do I prevent stage fright when I give a presentation?
■   How do I keep control of a meeting when people are arguing?
■   How can I get through the reading I have to do more efficiently?

FEEDBACK

The first part of the activity asked you to apply the theoretical ideas discussed in this section to a particular form of communication. This exercise should have added to your confidence and, hopefully, will also increase your effectiveness. The second part of the activity asked you to identify your personal learning needs in relation to this method of communication. Keep these needs in mind when you are working through the relevant section of the book. (You may also develop skills in other areas of communication which you can transfer to the area where you feel most in need of development.)

Summary

Now that you have finished this section you should be able to:

- describe a basic model of communication
- provide and ask for effective feedback
- identify the purpose of your communication
- prioritize the contents of your communication
- consider the needs of your audience
- communicate at an appropriate time
- choose an appropriate channel of communication

Section 2 Listening and talking

A lot of people talk too much and listen too little. They forget that communication is a two-way process. In most situations, it is actually more useful to be a good listener than a good speaker.

In the first part of this section you will practise some methods of helping other people to get their message across to you. You will also explore techniques you can use to make sure that your communication has been received and understood and also to guide a conversation along the lines you want it to follow.

The second part of the section explores how you can use your talking and listening skills on the telephone.

Listening skills

The people whom we think of as the best communicators are in actual fact often the people who are the best listeners.

ACTIVITY 13

Think of someone – either a colleague or someone you know outside work – whom you always enjoy talking to. Which of these statements are true of this individual?

		True	False
1	Things often seem a lot clearer after I've spoken to him/her.	❑	❑
2	He/she always seems interested in what I've got to say.	❑	❑
3	He/she is so entertaining, I don't have to contribute much to the conversation.	❑	❑
4	I find it easy to explain things to him/her.	❑	❑
5	He/she is very quick at picking things up.	❑	❑

You probably decided that all of these statements are true, except for number 3. The conversations we enjoy most are those in which we feel that our own contribution is heard and understood by the other person. These are the conversations in which true communication takes place.

Listening is an active, not a passive, process. A good listener does not simply absorb everything that is said without comment, but helps the speaker to articulate and explain his or her ideas. This benefits the listener, who gains an understanding of what is being said. It can also help the speaker to gain new insights into what he or she is saying.

Active listening involves using both non-verbal and verbal techniques.

NON-VERBAL TECHNIQUES FOR ACTIVE LISTENING

You can tell when someone isn't listening to you. Their eyes wander around the room, they fidget or shift uneasily from foot to foot. You may not be consciously aware of the signals that the person you are talking to is giving off, but they have a very powerful effect. It is extremely difficult to talk to someone if you feel you haven't got their attention. Good listeners use a variety of non-verbal techniques to indicate that they are taking in what is being said.

Eye contact

Look directly at the person who is speaking to you. This indicates that you are interested in hearing what he or she is saying. It will also allow you to pick up extra clues about the speaker's meaning. It is not necessary, or even desirable, to maintain direct eye contact throughout a conversation. In Western society, it is usual for the listener to look at the speaker more than the speaker looks at the listener.

Smiles and facial expressions

Smiles indicate that you are open to hearing what is being said. Also allow yourself to react to the emotional content of what the other person is saying. If you mirror the expression on the speaker's face, this will convey that the message is getting across.

Posture

If you lean forwards in your chair, this is interpreted as a sign that you listening. If you tilt your head sideways this has a similar effect. Slight nods of the head indicate that you are following what is being said. If you mirror the posture of the person who is speaking, this conveys that you are sympathetic to what they are saying. If you are standing or sitting, the angle between your body and the body of the speaker indicates how much of your attention you are giving to the conversation.

Distracting movements

Try to keep your hands still. Don't doodle with a pen or fiddle with your watchstrap when you are listening. It implies that your attention is elsewhere.

Watching the speaker's body language

You can often tell more about what somebody means by watching their body language than by listening to the words. When people are saying things which are particularly important to them, their muscles can get tense, or they may glance at you to gauge your reaction.

A: So, how is the new project going?
B: Oh, fine. Up to schedule. Things are looking good. The clients are very happy about how things are moving. [B glances at A quickly.] And of course we're moving into the new offices next month...

In this example, B is wondering whether A has heard about the fact that the clients threatened to pull out last week unless major changes were made to the quality specifications.

ACTIVITY 14

The next time you are in a pub, on a train, or in some other public place where people talk to each other, observe the body language of those around you. Without listening to what is being said, how much can you tell about how a conversation is going? Are the people you are observing really communicating? How can you tell?

FEEDBACK

You will probably notice other signals which indicate how well people are communicating. Look at how people move their eyebrows and the position in which they hold their arms. Also be aware of various types of non-verbal signals that people from other cultures use. Discreet observation of other people is an excellent way to improve your own sensitivity to body language.

Using body language

You can use your own body language to indicate that a speaker has your attention. This helps the speaker to focus his or her mind and get to the point quickly. Positive body language can also be used when you disagree with what you are hearing. If you are giving positive signals, the speaker will probably feel less personally threatened, and therefore less ready to argue, when you question their words. There may also be times when you want to indicate strong disapproval or impatience. If you have been giving positive signals, and then discontinue them, this has a powerful effect.

The best way to start using body language consciously is to monitor your existing behaviour. Begin by trying to avoid giving out negative signals, then experiment with adopting positive body language. It is relatively easy to control your movements from the neck down, but much more difficult to control your facial expression. It is important not to be too ambitious here. If you put an exaggerated smile or frown on your face to indicate sympathy with what you are hearing, you will probably look both ridiculous and insincere. The interesting thing is, however, that if you remember to sit or stand in an attentive posture, you will actually **feel** more involved in the conversation. You can then let your face reflect your genuine reactions to what is being said.

VERBAL TECHNIQUES FOR ACTIVE LISTENING

You can also indicate your attention in a one-to-one discussion by what you say. There are several techniques which you should have at your disposal.

Encouraging

When you want a speaker to tell you more, it can be useful to prompt them occasionally with a simple 'Yes', 'Right', or 'Mmm'. You will often find that people pause slightly to let you make signals like this.

Silence

From time to time you will ask a question that the person you are speaking to finds difficult to answer. Instead of coming in quickly with another question, it can sometimes be productive to pause and wait for the other person to say more.

A: Why do you think we lost that order?
B: I don't know really ... It's hard to say...

[PAUSE]

B: I suppose it might have something to do with the things that Colin was talking about at the meeting last week ...

Paraphrasing

This is a way of checking that you understand what is being said. It involves repeating the essence of what has been said in your own words. It shows the speaker that you have been listening and may enable them to clarify their thoughts.

A: Yes, we are very happy indeed with the figures. Ten thousand last month, fifteen thousand this month and we are expecting to sell at least twenty thousand next month.
B: So you're looking at a month-on-month rise of 5000?
A: Yes, I suppose we are.

Reflecting

Reflecting is very similar to paraphrasing. It involves echoing the last part of what has been said in your own words.

A: The trouble is, Sally was absolutely brilliant with the customers and I'm finding it very hard to find a replacement of the same calibre.
B: Someone with similar skills.
A: That's right. I mean, Sally really was quite unique.

Paraphrasing and reflecting are helpful techniques. They show you are following the speaker's train of thought and prevent the conversation from turning into a monologue.

You have probably heard people who interject into conversations like this:

A: Of course, we never had this difficulty when we bought everything from Bennetts.
B: From Bennetts.

A: Because they always sent a rep along to help with the installation.

B: Help with the installation.

This kind of echoing is very irritating to listen to. Avoid simply parroting the speaker's final words, but try to add something to the dialogue when you paraphrase or reflect.

Summarizing

In a more formal conversation, it can be useful to sum up what has been said so far. This can help clarify a complicated discussion and is a good technique in situations where it is important that both parties share the same under-standing of what has been agreed. It is also an effective way to signal that one part of a discussion is over and it is time to move on to a new topic.

A: Monday and Tuesday were chaotic because of the end of the month. And on Wednesday we had to spend the entire afternoon listening to a health and safety talk. On Thursday my PA was away sick and on Friday Frank and Morris were up in Stockport.

B: So what you are saying is that you haven't been able to make much progress this week. What about the letter you sent to customers? Have you had any response from that?

Referring to things said earlier

If you can remember and repeat things that people have said in the past, they will be convinced that you are taking a close interest in what they have to say. Sales representatives sometimes make use of this technique, making notes on any personal details that potential customers let slip and referring to them in subsequent encounters. You can use a similar technique in other types of conversations. Here are some examples:

'Didn't you mention earlier that the control button sometimes got stuck on this model?'

'I remember you saying that the hotel you used in York was particularly good.'

'Last time we talked, didn't you tell me about a similar incident with the Accounts Department?'

'Is that the same as the questionnaire which you were describing earlier?'

Most people will be surprised and flattered that you remember details of what they have said. This technique is also useful if you suspect that the person you are talking to is trying to confuse or mislead you. For example:

A: I'm sorry, but there's nothing I can do if the parts haven't arrived. It'll take a full day to get the machine reassembled once we get the parts on site. You're not going to get this machine working again this side of the weekend.

B: Didn't you mention something once about a supplier in Birmingham who was offering 24 hour delivery on spare parts?

A: Did I? Oh, yes. Well, I suppose we could give them a try.

B: If you telephoned now, we could get the parts by the end of tomorrow. You estimated it would take a day to reassemble the machine, so we could be up and running again by Friday morning.

In this situation, B will not make herself popular with A, but will probably have increased his respect for her.

ACTIVITY 15

You will need a friend or colleague to help you with this activity. Practise using verbal and non-verbal signals to indicate that you:

1   are very interested in what the other person is saying
2   want to move on to another topic
3   are very bored with listening to the other person

Take turns at listening and speaking. Then answer these questions.
How did it feel to be on the receiving end of these signals?

1

2

3

Which techniques were most effective?

Which techniques did you feel most comfortable using?

You may have learned many different things from this activity. Here are some comments from other managers:

When my colleague tried to move me on to another topic, I suddenly realized that people give me that kind of signal all the time, and I hadn't been picking up the message. It made me think that perhaps I have a tendency to go on a bit sometimes.

I found it hard to interject and summarize. I realized this is because my body language is saying 'Carry on talking'.

I was surprised at the strength of my reaction when my partner was giving me signals that she was bored. I started to make exaggerated statements, and I was talking a lot louder, just to get her attention. I actually began to feel rather aggressive.

Until you are confident, it is a good idea to practise using these techniques in situations where the outcome is not important.

Saying what you mean

Many English people find it quite uncomfortable to speak plainly. They feel they are being rude if they use words which express exactly what they mean. For example, a manager might say to his PA:

'I wonder if you would mind finding that address for me when you've got a moment.'

when he actually means:

'I need that address now.'

Or, a director might respond to a proposal in a meeting by saying:

'You've done a marvellous job putting that proposal together, but I'm a little concerned that it might be slightly over-ambitious at the present time.'

when she really means:

'We can't afford it.'

If you are communicating with people who can de-code what you are saying, this courteous way of talking is acceptable. Many people expect to be spoken to in this way and would actually be insulted if you started expressing yourself more directly.

However, there are certain situations where it can cause problems. People from countries with different conventions about polite speech can be enormously frustrated by a conversation with an English person. They feel they never get a straight answer. Be aware of this when you are talking to people from abroad – there may be times when you have to express yourself more clearly.

Many people use indirect language in situations where they are worried about the reaction they are going to get. By being over-polite or saying things in a roundabout way, they hope to avoid a hostile response. They may say:

'We are unfortunately in the position where we have to let you go.'

or

'We feel that you would benefit from wider experience of the industry at this point in your career.'

or

'We are undertaking a de-layering exercise.'

or

'We would like to place your contract on a consultancy basis.'

These are just a few of the ways of telling someone that he or she has lost his job. You have probably heard of several other versions. If you have to give bad news, it shows more respect to the other person if you do it more directly. For example

'I'm sorry, but we are making you redundant.'

or

'I'm afraid that we cannot renew your contract.'

This way, the receiver can take in the news immediately. He or she is not placed in the embarrassing position of struggling to understand your meaning, and can concentrate on coming to terms with your message.

Speaking directly is also important in other, less extreme situations. For example, if you are talking to people who want to interpret what you say in their own way, you must pick your words very carefully.

ACTIVITY 16

You may have experienced a telephone conversation like this:

Sales representative: Good to hear your voice, John! Now, it's been a few months since I've been in the area and I've got one or two new products which I think you'll be very interested in seeing. When could I come in and give you a demonstration?

Busy executive: Oh, I'm not sure, I'm very tied up all this week. It's difficult to find a time. Perhaps I could get back to you.

Sales representative: What are you doing next Wednesday morning?

Busy executive: Well, it's not a good day, I've got meetings all morning...and more in the afternoon.

Sales representative: I'll come and take you out to lunch.

Busy executive: Oh, all right then.

What could this executive have said to avoid being manipulated into seeing the sales representative?

FEEDBACK

Ideally, the executive should not have taken this call in the first place. It would have been better if he had been protected from it by an administrator or an answering machine. However, once he had picked up the telephone, he should have answered the first question by saying, 'No, I'm sorry, I can't make an appointment to see you.' By appearing to limit his refusal to the present week, he provides information which the sales representative can turn to his advantage. By being defensive, he allows the representative to take the initiative in the situation.

The executive in the activity needed to be more assertive. This usually means using direct language, so that there is no possibility of your message being misinterpreted. Being assertive does not mean being aggressive or rude. It involves saying what you mean – and meaning what you say.

Questions

Questions are an essential tool in one-to-one discussions. They can serve many different purposes:

- to obtain information
- to express interest in a topic or an individual
- to get someone interested in a topic

- to find out someone's attitudes, knowledge or opinions
- to encourage critical thinking

There are several different types of questions which you can use.

CLOSED QUESTIONS

These questions ask for an answer from a narrow range of options, often simply 'yes' or 'no'. For example:

'Did you remember to put that order in?'
'Is Mr Patel arriving at 10 or 10.30?'
'Are you going to phone him, or shall I do it?'

If you ask a closed question, you are likely to get a very brief reply. These questions are not helpful if you want someone to enlarge on a topic. For example:

A: Was Richard interested in your proposal?
B: No, not really.

If A wants to find out more about Richard's reactions, she will have to ask supplementary questions. If she continues to ask closed questions, she will only be able to extract the information she wants a little at a time. The conversation may begin to feel like an interrogation.

Closed questions are useful if you are clarifying details.

A: So I turn the machine on at the wall and wait for the light to come on. Is it the green light or the red light?
B: The green light.

They can also be helpful if you want to pin somebody down. For example:

'If we increased our offer by £5000, would you accept?'

OPEN QUESTIONS

These are questions which can be answered in a number of ways. They usually begin with one of these words:

- Who?
- How?
- What?
- Why?
- When?
- Where?

It is usually impossible to reply to an open question with a one- or two-word answer.

A: What did Richard say when you mentioned your proposal?

B: Oh, he said it was an interesting idea, but we just don't have the funds available for any further capital investment until next year.

Open questions are a good way to get people to volunteer information or express their opinions. They can also be useful when you want to check that you have got your message across. For example:

'I would imagine we are all going to have to make some changes to take this new directive on board. Marsha, how would you see things working out in your department?'

ACTIVITY 17

Turn each of these closed questions into an open question.

1   Do you need any help with that?

2   Is that all right with you?

3   Did you change the supplier because you weren't happy with the prices?

FEEDBACK

Possible answers are:

1   What can I do to help you with that?
2   How do you react to that?
3   Why did you change the supplier?

It is quite easy to think of open questions, but much more difficult to remember to use them when you are talking to people. Many people find it easier to ask closed questions than open questions. This can be because they only want a limited amount of information or, sometimes, because they are nervous of the answer they may get to an open question.

There are occasions on which each type of question is appropriate.

'How would you feel about my changing the closing date?'

might be a suitable question at the start of a discussion, while at the end of the conversation, it might be right to use a closed question to clarify and confirm what has been said:

'Are we agreed that I change the closing date?'

Chunking up and chunking down

Sometimes you may want to lead a discussion away from general principles towards specific details. Or you may want to move in the opposite direction, so that the big picture emerges. The phrases 'chunking up' and 'chunking down' come from computer terminology. Open questions are a good way to achieve a change of direction of this kind.

Chunking up is useful when you feel a discussion is in danger of going off down the wrong track. For example, you can use it to restrain someone from telling you too many details about their own experience, without giving offence:

A: Take me, for instance. I came into this company with two 'O' levels to my name. English and Woodwork, that's all the qualifications I had when I started out. I didn't go to university. I didn't even stay on at school to do 'A' levels. We couldn't afford it. But I took every training course that my section leader recommended. I studied in my own time every evening for seven years ... and look at me today!

B: What value do you think that psychometric testing might have as part of our selection procedure?

Chunking down is useful when you want to focus on the implementation of ideas.

'If we were to use psychometric tests, how would we screen applicants first?'

You can actually use chunking up and chunking down to lead a discussion in any direction you want:

A: The clients were delighted with the prototypes we showed them.

B: So, how are things going with the project? [chunking up]

A: Oh, pretty well.

B: How did you resolve that difficulty you had with costs? [chunking down]

ACTIVITY 18

You will need a friend or colleague to help you with this activity. Decide on a topic which you want to discuss, but which your friend or colleague would rather avoid. (Keep this activity as light-hearted as you can – don't choose a subject which is really important to either of you.)

1   Practise using chunking up and chunking down to lead the conversation on to the topic you want to discuss.
2   Write some notes on how successful you were in using this technique

FEEDBACK

If you are skilled at using chunking up and chunking down, the other person will not see the direction in which your questions are leading – or if they do see where the discussion is heading, they will be powerless to stop it.

QUESTIONS TO AVOID

There are some types of question which are usually counterproductive.

Leading questions

These are questions which contain an assumption about the answer you are expecting:

'You can see the potential benefits to the company in this scheme, can't you?'

'You're not going to sign that, are you?'

'Surely you told him it was out of the question?'

A leading question tells the other person what you think about the subject. It reveals your own hand. This can make it difficult for him or her to express a different opinion without risking a conflict of some sort. Rather than disagree openly, people may give a non-committal answer or even tell a direct lie, and you will not find out what is really going on.

Compare this version:

A: You didn't breathe a word to Stavros about Carol being late in, did you?
B: No, of course not.

with this:

A: Did you say anything to Stavros?
B: What about?
A: About Carol being late in.
B: Well, he asked where she was and I had to say I hadn't seen her.

You may get someone to agree with you if you use leading questions, but the agreement may not be worth very much, if it is contrary to his or her real feelings about the matter. Also, if the person you are talking to does not answer in the way you expect, the temperature of the exchange may be raised unnecessarily.

A: Didn't you think Sasha did an absolutely fantastic job at the presentation?
B: Well, no, actually. I didn't.
A: Really? You weren't impressed?
B: No I wasn't. I thought her delivery was weak and her choice of OHPs was absolutely appalling.

Multiple questions

A multiple question is one in which there is more than one question posed at once. Often, an open question is followed up with a closed question.

'How is John settling down? Is he getting on all right with Brian?'

Multiple questions can confuse the person you are talking to, because they don't know which question to answer. You can also be confused by the reply, because you may not be able to tell which question has been answered.

A: How is John settling down? Is he getting on all right with Brian?
B: Oh, John's doing OK.

Does this mean that John is settling down well or that he is getting on with Brian?

Using the telephone

A manager needs a telephone. It is an essential tool. If your telephone is ever out of order, you probably feel isolated and powerless. But how effectively do you use your phone?

ACTIVITY 19

Monitor your use of the telephone for a day. Make two charts like these and keep them by the phone. Every time you receive or make a call, time it and fill in the appropriate chart.

At the end of the day, fill in the right-hand column of each chart.

Date:			
Calls received			
From whom	Time taken	Result	Was it worth the time?
Date:			
Calls made			
To whom	Time taken	Result	Was it worth the time?

FEEDBACK

If your record showed any of these things:

- You repeated phone calls with the same person on the same topic
- Most of your calls didn't justify the amount of time they took up
- You could not identify a result for some of your calls

then you will find it worthwhile developing your telephone skills.

On the telephone, you can't see the person you are talking to. This has both disadvantages and advantages. The main drawback is that you can't always tell how the other person is reacting to what you are saying. Is he or she busily taking notes? Looking bored? Or puzzled? Or sceptical? Or angry? You often can't tell whether the other person is in a **position** to give you their attention. Are they alone, or in the middle of talking to someone else? Are they in a crowded office where they may be overheard, or in a private space?

You have to compensate for the lack of visual information you are getting by being more explicit in your verbal communication. If you want to discuss something which will take several minutes to cover, or is of a confidential nature, ask the other person if this is a good time to talk.

Don't assume that the other person has understood your message – or that you have understood what they are telling you. Check understanding by:

- asking questions
- repeating what you hear
- asking the other person to repeat details

At the end of the call, summarize the action that is going to be taken:

> 'So, I'll have a word with Sally this afternoon about bringing the schedule forward, and you'll get back to me tomorrow morning with some alternative prices.'

On the other hand, the lack of visual contact on the telephone does have several advantages. You can speak to people from your own workspace, with your papers about you and with access to your own computer. Also, even if you are not very skilled at controlling your body language, it is relatively easy to control your voice and what you say – and convey the impression that you want. Maximize these benefits by having all the necessary information to hand before you make, or return, a call. Also consider the impression you want to give before you pick up the phone.

MAKING CALLS

Before you make a call, decide exactly what you want to get out of it.

Think of three calls you made yesterday. Did you want:

	1	2	3
■ a decision	❑	❑	❑	❑
■ to give information	❑	❑	❑	❑
■ to obtain information	❑	❑	❑	❑
■ to persuade someone	❑	❑	❑	❑
■ to give instructions	❑	❑	❑	❑
■ to receive instructions	❑	❑	❑	❑
■ something else?			

FEEDBACK

The clearer you are about your objectives before you make a call, the better. Make a list of the points you need to cover, and tick them off as you talk.

Prepare a call sheet with the following outline, which you fill in before and during the making of a call. It will:

■ help you plan your call in advance

■ provide a record which you can file with relevant papers and refer to again

Call to:
Date:
Time:
Subject:
Main points of call:
Related paperwork:
Notes of call:
Action:

When you make the call, state your purpose as soon as possible. For example:

'Gerry, I was hoping to discuss the agenda for the departmental meeting. Have you got five minutes to talk?'

If the other person is unable to have the conversation now, arrange a time when **you** will ring back.

Sometimes, you may have to ring an organization without a clear idea of whom you should speak to. In this situation, work out how you can explain what you want so that it can be understood by someone without specialist knowledge. For example, if you have a technical query, it is no good describing it to the switchboard operator. He or she will probably have no idea what you are talking about. If you know which department will be able to answer your question, ask to be put through to it. If you don't know how the organization you are ringing is structured, ask to speak to customer relations or public relations. The people who answer the phone in these departments will have a knowledge of their organization and be able to direct your enquiry. They will also probably have received training in answering the telephone and will handle your call efficiently.

When you make a call, think about the impression you want to create. Don't just reach for the phone as you sit hunched over your desk. Sit up straight, or stand up, before you dial. Smile, as though you were about to meet someone face-to-face. These preparations will be reflected in your tone of voice.

TAKING CALLS

Only take calls when you can deal with them. If you are too busy to answer the phone, arrange for it be answered by someone else who will take a message. Or put it on an answerphone. If this is not possible, **as soon as possible** in the conversation, ask your caller if you can ring him or her back. The more the caller says before you ask, the ruder the request sounds, because this suggests that it is a personal response to the caller, or what he or she is saying.

If you don't have the information to answer a query, arrange a time when you, or the person who has phoned you, will ring back. Remember that the person who makes the return phone call is in a stronger position.

Don't do anything else when you are answering the phone. It is extremely irritating if you hear the person you are speaking to:

- trying to talk to someone else in the room
- shuffling papers
- eating
- fiddling with their computer keyboard

Give the person who calls your full attention. If you can't do this, arrange another time to talk.

Make notes of phone calls you receive. You may like to use a chart similar to the one you use for outgoing calls. At the very least, make notes on each call on a separate sheet of paper which can be filed with the relevant documents.

At the end of the call, make sure you, and the caller, are both clear about what is going to happen next.

Summary

Now that you have finished this section you should be able to:

- use verbal and non-verbal techniques for active listening
- use open and closed questions in appropriate situations
- avoid ineffective types of questions
- use appropriate verbal techniques on the telephone
- make phone calls effectively
- receive phone calls effectively

Section 3 Writing and reading

If you are in conversation with someone and hear something you don't under-stand, you can usually ask the other person to explain what he or she means. And if the person you are talking to doesn't follow **your** meaning, you may find yourself asked for further explanations. In the previous section you prac-tised some of the techniques you can use to check that verbal messages have been received.

When you put a message in writing, you don't have the same oppor-tunities to check that your meaning has got across. If you haven't expressed yourself clearly, you may find that the person on the receiving end does one of the following:

- the wrong thing
- the right thing in the wrong way
- nothing at all

If you can't communicate clearly in writing, your effectiveness as a manager is severely limited. In this section we explore how you can get your message across on the page. We will look at some general principles which will help you in any kind of writing and also examine some types of document which have their own conventions.

Why are you writing?

From time to time, you will have probably received written communications like these:

- a report which uses technical language which is only accessible to experts in the field, or which does not back up its recommendations with the necessary facts
- a form which has been completed incorrectly
- a letter which fails to convince you that an organization has taken your complaint seriously
- a memo about a meeting which is sent out so late that it is impossible for you to attend, or which fails to alert you to an important item on the agenda

■ a description of a training course which is written in such convoluted language that you are unable to tell whether it would be useful to you or not

■ a reminder about a bill you have forgotten to pay, or have actually paid, which is phrased so rudely that you never want to use the company again

Each of these communications failed because the writer was unclear about what he or she wanted to achieve.

Before you write anything at work, pause for a moment and think about this question:

What do I want to happen as a result of this communication?

ACTIVITY 21

Think about the last six communications you wrote at work. In the boxes below, identify these communications and describe what you wanted to happen as result.

Try to keep your answers inside the boxes.

1

2

3

4

5

6

FEEDBACK

We restricted the space you had available in this activity because we wanted you to focus on the core purpose of each piece of communication. Here are some sample answers, based on the examples at the beginning of the section:

1	report on viability of new project: I wanted senior management to agree to fund the project

2	letter answering customer complaint: I wanted the customer to use the company again

3	expenses form: I wanted the accounts department to reimburse me for a hotel bill

4	memo giving details of a meeting: I wanted everyone involved to come to the meeting properly prepared

5	article in newsletter on a new training scheme: I wanted staff who might benefit to contact me for more details

6	letter asking a long-standing customer to settle an invoice: I wanted the customer to pay quickly and to buy from us again

Whatever the topic of your communication, you should be able to sum up its core purpose (what you want to happen as a result) in a very few words. If you can't do this, it is possible that you are not sufficiently clear about your reason for writing – and this lack of clarity will probably have been reflected in what you wrote. Once you have identified what you want to happen, you have the key to what you write and how you write it.

Content

All trainee journalists are taught a verse of poetry by Rudyard Kipling:

I keep six honest serving men
They taught me all I knew.
Their names are What? and Why? and When?
And How? and Where? and Who?

Journalists use these six questions to remind them of the information they should include in an article. You have probably seen items (almost) like this in your local paper, which show that the writer had these questions in mind:

Southwark pensioner Amy Smith, 73, was awoken by a loud noise at 6 am on Friday morning. She was surprised to see the legs of amateur parachutist Fred Jones, 35, protruding from the ceiling of the bedroom at her house in Warner Road, Camberwell ...

You can use the six journalist's questions as prompts when you are planning the content of any type of written communication.

For example, if you were sending out a memo inviting people to a presentation, you might need to include information on:

- **who** will be speaking and who will be invited to the presentation
- **what** the subject of the presentation will be
- **why** it is important that they attend
- **where** the presentation will be held
- **when** it will be held
- **how** they can get there

ACTIVITY 22   D4.4

Use the journalist's questions to plan the content of a memo asking for other managers' views on a proposal you are putting forward which will affect them.

- who?

- what?

- why?

- where?

- when?

- how?

FEEDBACK

Your answer may be similar to this:

- **who** you are consulting about your proposal
- **what** the proposal involves
- **why** you have put forward the proposal, and why you need their feedback
- **where** you would like them to give their feedback, such as in a meeting, by filling in a form or by contacting you personally
- **when** you need them to respond
- **how** your proposal will affect them

You may have interpreted the questions slightly differently to this, but they should have provided a reminder of the kinds of questions which people might need answers to.

When you are writing something important, it helps to show it to someone else and see if they have any questions. If you can't do this, try to leave a little time between writing and sending your document. If you come back to it with a clear mind and look at it again, you can often spot things you have left out.

Draw a mind map

This is another technique you can use to plan the content of what you write. It was developed by Tony Buzan, who has written several books on the subject.

1 Begin by writing the topic in the middle of a large piece of paper
2 Then write key words relating to different aspects of the topic around the centre
3 Working outwards, subdivide your headings
4 Make connections where you see them

It doesn't matter how untidy the result is, as long as it makes sense to you.

A mind map is a good way to get an overview of a topic. Once you have all your thoughts down on one piece of paper, you can find the most logical structure to arrange them for your readers.

FINDING A STRUCTURE

Journalists always put their most important points first, because they know they must catch the reader's attention quickly and people may not read on to the end of the article.

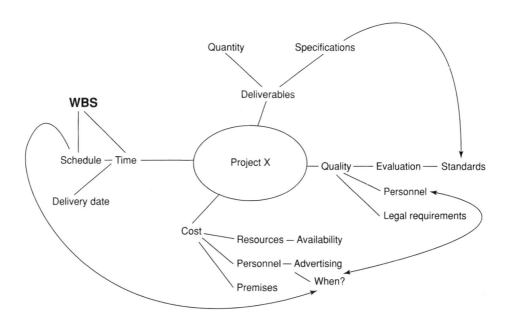

Figure 1 A mind map

There are several ways in which you can structure a piece of writing.

Telling a story

Sometimes it is appropriate to describe things in the order they happened – or in the order you would like them to happen. You can use this structure if you are writing an account of an accident or drafting a briefing document describing the stages of a process. This is a simple structure for the reader to follow and can be very effective.

Arguing a case

Sometimes you need to persuade your readers to do something. In a report, you could use a structure like this:

- Option 1: reasons for and against
- Option 2: reasons for and against
- Option 3: reasons for and against

Or you could arrange your argument like this:

- Underlying issues and criteria for the decision
- Option 1: how it meets the criteria
- Option 2: how it meets the criteria
- Option 3: how it meets the criteria

In a report, it is important to give both sides of the argument, or your readers will not have confidence in your recommendations. There are also some situations where you do not have to give any counter-arguments.

Selling an idea

Copywriters use the word AIDA to plan the contents of their leaflets and advertisements.

- **A**ttention: First, get your readers' attention with an arresting image or slogan
- **I**nterest: Then show the readers why what you are writing is likely to interest them
- **D**esire: Create a desire for whatever it is you are trying to promote
- **A**ction: Provide something for the readers to do in response to what they have read

You can see this technique at work in most of the advertising material which you receive – and you can also use it yourself in many other business situations. For example, here is a memo asking staff to provide input into the reorganization of the office.

To all staff
From Jeff
Date: 2nd March

We are taking your desk away.

We are going to redecorate and refurnish the main office at the end of March. This will involve a major reorganization and will affect everyone who works in this room.

Before we finalize the plans, I need to know what you think would make your workspace more effective. Do you need more storage space? A quiet area away from the phones? Better access to other members of your workgroup?

I can't promise to meet everybody's requirements, but if you tell me what you want, I will do my best to reflect your needs in the plans.

Please complete the enclosed questionnaire and send it to me by noon this Friday, March 6th.

ACTIVITY 23

Analyse how this memo is put together. Mark the parts which perform these functions:

■ Attention
■ Interest
■ Desire
■ Action

FEEDBACK

You probably identified these parts of the memo:

■ Attention: We are taking your desk away
■ Interest: We are going to redecorate and refurnish the main office at the end of March. This will involve a major reorganization and will affect everyone who works in this room
■ Desire: Do you need more storage space? A quiet area away from the phones? Better access to other members of your workgroup?
■ Action: Please complete the enclosed questionnaire and send it to me by noon this Friday, March 6th

We will end this look at structure by considering some special types of document which you will probably have to write at some time or other.

LETTERS

You can use the AIDA formula in sales letters. Letters giving information can follow the OFAC pattern:

■ Occasion: Say why you are writing
■ Facts: Give information
■ Action: Make a request or a suggestion
■ Closing: Offer to provide more information

Whatever type of letter you are writing, if you are responding to another letter, or any other type of communication, you need to make this clear to the reader: For example:

'Thank you for your letter of 16th July.'

'In response to your telephone enquiry ...'

'Following the discussion at the meeting on Thursday 15th ...'

Most letters to organizations have to be stored in a filing system. It helps if you can give your letter a title, so that the recipient, and your own staff, can instantly see what it is about. If you want to cover more than one topic, consider sending two or more shorter letters, so that they can be filed and retrieved appropriately. Break your letter into short paragraphs, each dealing with a separate point.

Most organizations have their own house-style for the layout of letters, which you should follow. Many organizations have standard letters which can be adapted for different circumstances. These are obviously much quicker to write, but can feel very impersonal to receive.

ACTIVITY 24

Would you use a standard letter, if you had one available, in these circumstances?

		yes	no
1	responding to a request for a brochure	❑	❑
2	asking someone for interview	❑	❑
3	thanking someone for a large order	❑	❑
4	congratulating a member of staff	❑	❑
5	making someone redundant	❑	❑
6	giving warning of a disciplinary action	❑	❑

FEEDBACK

A standard letter would be adequate in situations 1 and 2, but could give offence in situations 3 and 4. In situations 5 and 6, the exact wording would be important from a legal point of view and you would be better to use a standard letter which had been passed by your organization's legal advisers.

PROPOSALS

A proposal is a document which attempts to sell an idea to the people who will fund it. There are two main kinds of proposal, and it is important to know which kind you are writing:

- proposals which are written in response to an invitation to tender
- proposals which are **not** written in response to an invitation to tender

In the first type of proposal, you do not have to sell the idea that something has to be done. Your readers already know that. They have identified a problem or an opportunity and have asked what you would do about it. Your job is to convince them that your particular proposal is the perfect answer for them.

In the second type of proposal, your readers may not realize that they have a problem or an opportunity at all. You have to convince them that they do need to do something and that your proposal, among all the courses of action they could adopt, is the best way forward.

Both types of proposal should provide most of the information your readers need to make their decision. You may follow your proposal up with a presentation or a meeting, but the main facts should be there in the original document. The facts you choose to present will be different, depending on which type of proposal you are writing.

Let's look first at a proposal which is written in response to an invitation to tender.

ACTIVITY 25

Imagine you run a small training company. You are responding to an invitation to tender for setting up a new training programme. What will the client want to know? Use the journalist's questions to decide what should go into your proposal

- who?

- what?

- why?

- where?

- when?

- how?

The client will want to know:

- who will be trained and who will do the training
- what qualification or level of training is involved
- how your particular package will benefit the organization
- where the training will take place
- when the training will happen and how long it will take
- how much it will cost and how it will be organized

There is no set formula that a proposal of this kind must take, but it should follow these rules:

- State clearly and concisely what you are proposing to do.
- Give brief reasons for these decisions, stressing the benefits.
- Give concrete details of costs, timescale, standards, etc.
- Address every area which your readers will be interested in.
- Use headings to help your readers find their way around.
- Keep your proposal as brief as possible

Aim to give your readers a clear picture of what it is they are agreeing to. You only need to give the arguments in favour of your proposal. It is up to other people to come up with the reasons why it should not happen in the way you suggest. Present the details of what you are proposing first, and then say why this is what should happen.

> '10 sessions will be necessary to cover the areas in which you are legally obliged to train your staff ... Mindset Training can offer you an existing training package which has been used successfully in 150 companies in the UK.'

If you are presenting a proposal in which you are attempting to sell a project which has not been asked for, you have to start by convincing your readers of the need to spend money. A good structure to use here is:

- Position: Describe the current position. This will help your readers understand the context in which to read your proposal
- Problem: Describe the problem or opportunity, backing up your assertion with hard evidence
- Possibilities: Discuss possible courses of action. Here, you should give the pros and cons for each option. Be as objective as you can, or your readers won't have confidence in the recommendation which follows
- Proposal: Recommend a course of action. Make what you are proposing absolutely clear. Think of all the aspects your readers will be interested in, such as time, cost, resources, etc. Answer obvious objections (although you needn't anticipate all the negative comments you may have to deal with). Back up your case with facts and figures

REPORTS

A report is probably the most lengthy – and the most daunting – document that you will have to write at work. Luckily, you will not be the first person to write a report for your organization. You can learn a lot from examples prepared by other people.

First, look at the structure which earlier reports use. It will probably contain most of these elements:

Title page

Summary

giving a quick synopsis of what the report says – for readers who are in a hurry

Contents page

useful in reports which are longer than six pages

Introduction

describing why the report was written, the terms of reference and methodology

Main report

the main body of the report – each section and paragraph should be numbered

Conclusions and recommendations

you can separate your conclusions from your recommendations if you wish

Acknowledgements

names of people and organizations you have consulted

References

giving details of any source material you have quoted or referred to in the text

Glossary

explaining technical terms, abbreviations or symbols used in the text

Appendices

giving supplementary information, such as survey results, plans or detailed calculations, which back up what you say in the main body of the report

Follow the structure which is usual within your organization, unless it is completely inappropriate for your own report.

Write the main body of your report first. In most reports each paragraph is numbered, so that they can be referred to easily in subsequent discussions. Once the main part of the report is finished, write your introduction and your conclusions and recommendations. Decide what supplementary evidence you want your readers to read and put it into the appendices. The preparation of the title page, contents list, acknowledgements, references and glossary are purely editorial tasks. Although they are time-consuming, they should not be difficult. Finally, write your summary. This is part of your report which people will look at first. It should provide a brief resumé of the main points you make in your report.

E-MAIL

The big advantage of e-mail is that you can deliver a written message directly onto someone's computer in a matter of seconds. E-mails can be sent from one side of an office to another, or across continents.

Keep e-mails as brief as possible. Remember that you are using them to save time. You can attach files to an e-mail, but you may lose formatting on documents unless the receiver has a similar computer to your own.

If you are referring to a previous e-mail, you can copy and quote the relevant parts.

Dear Michael

<<could you give me a reference for that book on accounts you mentioned at the meeting?>>

Certainly. The book was:

'Accounts Demystified: How to understand and use company accounts' by Anthony Rice, published by The Institute of Management Foundation and Pitman Publishing, 1993.

I can recommend it!

Yours

Chris

It is considered impolite to write in capitals in an e-mail,

BECAUSE IT LOOKS AS IF YOU ARE SHOUTING!

Some people use combinations of symbols to convey emotions. Turn your head sideways to look at these examples:

:-) means that you are smiling

:- (means that you are not happy

Dozens of these emoticoms exist – and some of them are very silly indeed. Acronyms are also used a lot in e-mail. Here are few of the most common ones:

AFAIK	As Far As I Know
BFN	Bye For Now
BTW	By The Way
FYI	For Your Information
g	grin – usually <g> or [g]
HSIK	How Should I Know
IANAL	I Am Not A Lawyer
IMHO	In My Humble Opinion

LOL	Laughing Out Loud
NOYB	None Of Your Business
OIC	Oh, I See
TANSTAAFL	There Ain't No Such Thing As A Free Lunch
TIA	Thanks In Advance

You may have to decipher messages written in this way. Don't use these emoticoms and acronyms yourself, unless you are **absolutely certain** that the person on the receiving end will understand and appreciate them.

Remember that the purpose of communication is to get a message across, not to puzzle or impress your reader.

Style

In business, keep your language plain and simple. You will find that it is much quicker to write in this way – and your readers will find it much easier to absorb your message.

People who do not use plain and simple language usually do it for one of the following reasons:

- They are copying a writing style that is used by other people in the organization
- They have not got a firm grasp of grammar
- They are unclear about what they are trying to communicate
- They think that long words and complicated sentences will impress people
- They have an inflated idea of their own importance

None of these is an acceptable reason for using language which is difficult to read. The **only** situations in which you need to use technical language or complicated sentence structures are when:

- technical words are essential to convey your meaning and you know they will be readily understood by your audience

  or

- there are contractual or other legal reasons why a particular form of words has to be used.

These situations come up much less often than most people imagine. Many organizations, including government agencies such as the Inland Revenue, are now making strenuous efforts to simplify and clarify their written communications with the public. Increasingly, the value of plain, clear English is being appreciated **within** organizations, too.

KEEPING IT PLAIN AND SIMPLE

Your aim when writing should be to find the simplest and most concise way to express your thoughts. The following guidance should help.

Write short sentences

Short sentences are easier to read than long ones. You will find that they are also much easier to write. In a short sentence, you do not have to worry about complicated grammatical structures or difficult punctuation.

ACTIVITY 26

Look at a piece of writing which you have produced recently. How long are your sentences, on average?

FEEDBACK

Generally, you should aim for an average of about 15–20 words per sentence. If your average sentence length is shorter than this, your writing may feel disconnected and jerky. If your average is higher, you may be making things unnecessarily difficult for your readers.

One reason that people write long sentences is because they try to make each sentence convey too much information. It is not necessary to express a complex idea in a single sentence – your meaning may actually be much clearer if you divide your sentences up.

ACTIVITY 27

Rewrite this long sentence so that it is easier to read:

Although the promotion was not as successful as we hoped it was going to be, we did achieve significant results at the younger end of the market and these results, when viewed alongside the data provided by our earlier survey, have given us the necessary encouragement, subject to the agreement of the committee, to develop the product further, which we now propose to do along the lines suggested in the recommendations made at the meeting held at Head Office in January.

FEEDBACK

This version is much easier to read:

The promotion was not as successful as we hoped it was going to be. However, we did achieve significant results at the younger end of the market. These results, when viewed alongside the data from our earlier survey, encourage us to develop the product further. If the committee agrees, we therefore propose to follow the recommendations made at the meeting held at Head Office in January.

You may also notice that, in the second version, several unnecessary words have been removed.

Use short words and phrases

Many people believe that long words and phrases make what they have to say sound more interesting and impressive. At school, we were all encouraged to show the breadth of our vocabulary. Teachers like it when their pupils include difficult words in their essays because it shows they can spell them correctly. In the adult world of work, your readers are not interested in your command of the English language, but in the content of what you have to say. Short words and phrases will make your message come across more clearly.

ACTIVITY 28

Write a shorter word or phrase for each of these examples:

1 commencement _____

2 at your earliest convenience _____

3 conclusion _____

4 in addition to _____

5 purchase _____

6 utilize _____

7 with regard to _____

8 in the event of _____

9 facilitate _____

10 at the present moment in time _____

FEEDBACK

Compare your answers with these:

1 start

2 as soon as possible

3 end

4 as well as

5 buy

6 use

7 about

8 if

9 help

10 now

The length of your words and sentences provides a guide to the readability of your text. Many word processors will work out these calculations for you. Here is a simple readability test you can do yourself.

How to calculate your Fog Index

1 Work out your average sentence length. For example: 18

2 Count the number of long words (words with more than two syllables). Write this as a percentage of your total number of words. For example: 12%

3 Add these two figures together. For example: 18 + 12 = 30

4 Multiply the result by 0.4. For example: 30 x 0.4 = 12

This is your Fog Index. It is roughly equivalent to the number of years of full-time education that people will need to have had to read what you have written reasonably easily.

ACTIVITY 29

Work out the Fog Index for something you have written at work.

1 Average sentence length =

2 Percentage of long words =

3 Add the two figures together =

4 0.4 x   =

Did you write at the appropriate level for your audience?

FEEDBACK

These days, most people spend 12 years in full-time education. If you were writing for an audience who did not go on to further or higher education, your Fog Index should not have been higher than 12.

Write active sentences

Your writing will be much more immediate and lively if you use the active, instead of the passive, voice. In an active sentence, the main verb describes what somebody (or something) did (or is doing, or will do) to something (or someone) else:

- We **ran** the course
- She **will promote** him
- He **arranged** a meeting
- The report **describes** the problem

In a passive sentence, the main verb describes what was done (or is being done, or will be done) by something (or someone) to something (or someone) else.

- The course **was run** by us
- He **will be promoted** by her
- The meeting **was arranged** by him
- The problem **is described** in the report

Compare these two versions:

> 'Any comments which are received after this date cannot be taken into account.'
>
> 'We cannot take into account any comments which we receive after this date.'

The second version has much more impact.

ACTIVITY 30
Rewrite these examples as active sentences.

I   National awards have been won by several of our area representatives.

2   Components which fail to achieve the necessary standard will be rejected by the Checkers.

3   Although eight bids were submitted by UK companies, only two were examined by the committee.

FEEDBACK

Compare your answers with these:

I   Our area representatives have won several national awards.
2   The Checkers will reject components which fail to achieve the necessary standard.
3   UK companies submitted eight bids, but the committee only examined two of them.

There may be circumstances, such as when you are writing a formal report, where you will be expected to use the passive voice. Follow your organization's house-style for documents of this kind, but use the active voice in other situations.

Write positive sentences

It is very easy to get into the habit of expressing yourself in negative sentences, like these:

'It is unlikely that the meeting will continue after 3 pm.'
'Nobody is more aware than me of the difficulties this has caused.'
'Please do not park outside the designated area.'

Your meaning will come across more strongly, and you will offer fewer opportunities for misunderstanding, if you write positive statements, like these:

'The meeting will probably end by 3 pm.'
'I am very aware of the difficulties this has caused.'
'Please park inside the designated area.'

ACTIVITY 31

Check your own writing for positive and negative statements. Could you make your meaning clearer if you used positive sentences more frequently?

FEEDBACK

You don't have to turn all your sentences into positive statements! You may have found some sentences in your own writing where you will distort the meaning if you change them in this way. However, these will have more impact if, in general, you try to express yourself in positive statements.

Avoid jargon

If you are honest, there are probably times when you rather enjoy using the right jargon. Most people do. It is a way of showing that you are an 'insider' who can 'speak the language'. Using the right jargon is a powerful way of showing that you are a member of a group. As a means of communication, however, it is not particularly effective.

The problem with jargon is that, if you don't understand what it means, you may not have the courage to ask, because, if you do ask for clarification, you are revealing that you are not a member of the 'group'. In a situation where status and control are important, this may be the last thing that you want to do. As a result, many people use technical language inaccurately, because they have only the haziest idea of what it means. Jargon is particularly rife in management circles, where new buzzwords appear all the time.

There are times when it is appropriate to use technical language. In every type of work, there are some specialist words that express concepts which cannot easily be explained in ordinary vocabulary. Technical words are acceptable, as long as:

1   you could, if pressed, give a clear definition of what they mean
2   they really are the best way to convey what you mean
3   you are certain that your readers will understand them

If the technical words you want to use don't pass **all** of these three tests, you should find a different way to express your meaning, as this editor did:

I was looking at a design for a book the other day. I thought we needed to give more emphasis to the captions and so I wrote a note to the designer saying: 'Please print the captions over a 20% tint of the second colour, with a 2pt keyline.' When I sent the design to the author, I wanted to explain what would happen to the captions, but I expressed it differently. I said 'We will put the captions in light blue boxes.'

ACTIVITY 32

Fill in the table below. Find three examples of jargon which you have used recently in written communications at work. How would you explain these words in everyday language to someone without your specialist knowledge?

Jargon	Everyday language

FEEDBACK

If you found these definitions in ordinary language difficult, you may have been trying to give too much background information. Think about what a non-specialist reader **really** needs to know about the word, not what you could tell him or her.

When you are writing a report, your task is often to explain a technical subject to a non-technical audience. If you have to use words which you suspect your readers are unlikely to know, explain them. You may be able to do this in the text. For example:

'They measured the levels of the naturally produced chemical histamine, which plays an important role in the allergic response.'

If you can't explain technical terms as you use them, your readers may appreciate a glossary.

Also, when you use abbreviations, write the words in full the first time they occur, with the abbreviation in brackets. You can then use the abbreviation again without explaining it. For example:

'We sent the samples to the Central Biochemical Laboratory (CBL) for analysis. Four days later, the Director of the CBL contacted us to discuss the results.'

Many reports intended for the general public now contain a glossary of abbreviations.

Thinking about presentation

The way you present your writing matters. Compare these two examples:

SUCCESSIVE WAVES OF DOWNSIZING, CLOSURES AND REORGANIZATIONS PUT PRESSURE ON MANAGERS AND EMPLOYEES ALIKE. ADDITIONALLY, TECHNOLOGICAL CHANGES TO IMPROVE THE SPEED OF COMMUNICATIONS IN THE FORM OF FAX MACHINES, MOBILE TELEPHONES AND E-MAIL HAVE CREATED TWENTY-FOUR HOUR ACCESSIBILITY. THIS IS A POTENTIAL RECIPE FOR DISASTER.

Successive waves of downsizing, closures and reorganizations put pressure on managers and employees alike. Additionally, technological changes to improve the speed of communications in the form of fax machines, mobile telephones and e-mail have created twenty-four hour accessibility. This is a potential recipe for disaster.

The words are exactly the same, but the second version is much easier to read.

ACTIVITY 33

Can you identify six differences in the way the two versions are presented?

1

2

3

4

5

6

FEEDBACK

1   The most obvious difference is that the first version is printed completely in capitals, while
    the second version uses upper and lower case
2   The typeface is smaller in the first version
3   There is more space between the lines in the second version
4   The first version uses a sans-serif typeface (like this) while the second version uses a serif
    typeface (like this)
5   The line length is longer in the first version
6   In the first version, the text is justified, so that all the lines are exactly the same length. In the
    second version it is unjustified, with a ragged right-hand edge

These days, many managers have access to word processors and printers. You
may have to make decisions about the appearance of your work which would

once have been taken by professional typists or graphic designers. The following guidance should help:

- Text which is printed in capitals is much harder to read than text which is written in upper and lower case
- If you want people to read more than a few lines of text, don't use a typeface smaller than 10 pt.
- If you have to use a smaller typeface, extra space between the lines increases readability
- Unjustified text is more readable than justified text, where the gaps between the words are of variable length
- Serif typefaces are more readable than sans-serif typefaces.
- Set your line length so that there are between 7 and 12 words on each line

You can also provide extra signals and signposts to help your readers find their way around your text.

Headings

Headings allow your readers to find particular parts of your text quickly. They also give a context for the text which follows. In a long document, you can use a hierarchy of main and subheadings to make your structure clear.

Your headings should stand out from your text. Many people use a contrasting typeface, printed in a larger size. Although most wordprocessors give you the option of using many different typefaces, don't use more than two in any one document. A single typeface, used in bold or italic, in different sizes and with a different amount of space above and below it, can produce a surprisingly wide range of effects.

Resources
We must consider our underlying objects and tailor our use of resources

Resources
We must consider our underlying objects and tailor our use of resources

Resources
We must consider our underlying objects and tailor our use of resources

Resources
We must consider our underlying objects and tailor our use of resources

Remember to always leave more space above a heading than below it.

White space

You have probably seen full-page advertisements in the newspaper, which must have cost thousands of pounds, in which much of the page is completely empty, apart from a few words in the middle. It's a very impressive effect. Graphic designers are much bolder in using white space than other people are. The more space a block of copy has around it, the more it stands out – and the more important it seems. You can make your writing look much more professional if you don't try to crowd too much in. Leave wide margins and be courageous about using white space.

Different kinds of text

If your document contains different kinds of text, you can make this immediately obvious to the eye. For example, in this book, you can instantly tell whether you are reading an activity, ordinary text or a quotation. You may decide to justify parts of your text, or print it in a smaller or larger size. Or you may place a section of text inside a box, or put a shaded tint behind it. It is all right to have some parts of your document, such as your captions or footnotes, which are not quite as easy to read as your main text.

When all internal documents were typewritten, capitals or underlining were used for emphasis. These techniques now look very old fashioned. If you want to emphasize a particular word or phrase, use *italics* or **bold**.

If you want to make several linked points, you can number them, or use bullet points. This helps your reader see the connection between them.

Images

There are some things which are difficult to put into words. It is now relatively easy to include images with your text. They can help in several different ways.

ACTIVITY 34

Think of examples of images which fulfil each of these functions:

1 showing people how to do something

2 helping people recognize something quickly

3 affecting how people feel about something

4 helping people understand something

FEEDBACK

Compare your answers with these:

1 Diagrams and flowcharts are good at explaining processes. Maps show people how to get from A to B
2 Logos and symbols can convey a simple idea or help people make a connection very quickly
3 Photographs, illustrations and use of colour can all have an emotional effect
4 Cartoons can make a point in a humorous way. Diagrams can explain new ideas. Graphs can show the significance of figures much more clearly than charts and tables

It is a mistake to use graphic images in your writing just because you have the technology to include them. However, there may well be situations where you could use some of the ideas in the last activity to help get your message across to your readers.

ACTIVITY 35

Choose an internal document produced by your organization which you do not think is well presented. Use the techniques described in the last few pages to increase its impact.

FEEDBACK

If you improve the way you present your written communications, you may find your ideas spreading. Other people in your organization may start to copy your approach.

The process of writing

We will end this part of the section by bringing together the stages in the writing process. Use this checklist the next time you write something at work.

❑ Decide what you are trying to achieve

❑ Identify your audience – what do they need to know? What do they know already?

❑ Decide what you need to cover – the six journalist's questions or drawing a mind map will help

❑ Decide on your structure – are there any special conventions you should follow?

❑ Draft your document, remembering to keep your style simple and concise

❑ Decide how you will present your document. Is it legible? Does it have impact? Are you including graphic images? Have you given your readers as much help as possible?

❑ Check the content of your document. Have you left anything out? Is there anything you could cut out? Are your points in the most logical order?

❑ Check your writing style. Is your meaning clear? Is there anything your could express more simply? Check your spelling.

❑ Redraft your document. Do you need to show it to anyone before you send it?

❑ Send your document.

Reading

Everyone uses more than one reading technique.

ACTIVITY 36

Describe what you do in these situations:

1   You want to find a number in a telephone directory.

2   You receive a letter which will tell you whether or not your job application has been successful.

3   You are checking your insurance policy to see if you are covered for an accident.

FEEDBACK

1   When you look up a name in a telephone directory, you don't read every word on the page. You let your eyes scan quickly down the column of print until you find the name you are searching for.

2   When you open a letter like this, you skim through it quickly, looking for key phrases like 'delighted to offer you' or 'regret to inform you'. Once you've got a general impression of what it says, you read it more carefully.

3   When the details are important, you read slowly and carefully, thinking about the meaning of every sentence.

The three reading techniques which you use in ordinary life are:

■   scanning
■   skimming
■   careful reading

Effective reading involves choosing the most effective technique for any situation, and being able to switch between techniques when it is appropriate. The most common reason that people find reading a burden is that they feel obliged to read everything carefully. This is very time-consuming and usually quite unnecessary.

Most documents contain only a few key ideas that you will need to retain. Use scanning and skimming to identify them.

SQ3R

This is an approach to reading and notetaking which is taught to students. It is useful in many other contexts, too.

Survey

When you pick up a book, scan the contents page and decide if it is relevant to you. When you are looking at a report or an article, read the summary or abstract at the beginning. This will tell you if it is worth going further. Use the subheadings and any passages which are picked out in larger type to help find your way around. Use scanning and skimming to decide whether it is worth investing your time in going any further.

Question

Think of questions that you would like the author to answer for you in the text. This helps make reading an active process, in which you set the agenda.

Read

Read as much of the text as you need to answer your questions – and no more. Don't get side-tracked. As you read, constantly challenge the author with more questions and comments, like these:

- Can you back that up?
- That doesn't make sense
- Where did you get that idea from?
- I strongly disagree with you on that point
- That's a very neat solution!
- I'd like to see you try to make that work in this organization

Be as rude as you like. The more involved you become with what you are reading, the more you will remember.

Recall

Stop reading. Make notes on the main points you have read. Use your own words, not the author's words. Taking notes is an excellent way of increasing your concentration. If you are reading a document which you will have to take action on, mark your action points in a different colour.

Review

Leave your notes, then go back to them later and see if you still understand them. It is very easy to write notes which make perfect sense at the time, but are completely incomprehensible when you look at them later.

ACTIVITY 37

1 Find an article in a business journal that looks relevant to you. Use the SQ3R technique to make brief notes on its contents.
2 Read the article carefully, from beginning to end. Did you miss out anything important in your notes?

FEEDBACK

We hope that this activity will have convinced you of the value of the SQ3R technique. If you were not satisfied that your notes provided an accurate and useful record of what you read, decide how you should modify your technique.

DEALING WITH YOUR IN-TRAY

If reports and correspondence pile up in your in-tray, you may need to take a more proactive approach to reading. As soon as something arrives on your desk, look at it quickly and decide whether you are going to:

- do it
- dump it
- delegate it

ACTIVITY 38

Go through your in-tray, or think about what has arrived in it recently. Write three items in each column.

Do it	Dump it	Delegate
1	1	1
2	2	2
3	3	3

FEEDBACK

The sooner you can make this decision, the clearer your desk will be and the more in control you will feel. You will be able to see what you **really** ought to be spending your time on and will consequently be much more effective.

Put the 'dump it' pile in the waste-paper basket and pass the 'delegate' documents on. Use your scanning and skimming skills to organize your 'to do' pile into further categories:

- urgent and important
- urgent but not important
- important but not urgent
- not important and not urgent

This is the order in which you should tackle these documents. Read them as carefully as you need to and take the necessary action.

Summary

Now that you have finished this section you should be able to:

- clarify the purpose of a piece of writing
- plan the contents of a written communication
- use an appropriate structure for your writing
- write effective letters, proposals and reports
- use e-mail effectively
- use a clear and concise writing style
- calculate the readability of your writing
- present your writing to gain maximum impact
- use scanning, skimming and careful reading techniques in appropriate situations
- deal with the reading matter in your in-tray efficiently

Section 4 Meetings

Meetings are well known to be inefficient for both the dissemination of information and the communication of information. As a result, they are indispensable when one does not actually want to do anything but still give the appearance of working. Meetings can stifle ideas, help to postpone and prevaricate over difficult decisions. A committee meeting is often a cul-de-sac down which ideas are lured to their death.

You may not have such a cynical view of meetings as this[1], but you have probably attended quite a few of these occasions when you felt that your time – and the time of everyone else in the room – was wasted.

This section will help you to organize meetings that will achieve their objectives. It also explores some communication skills, which will be useful in negotiating meetings. You will look at ways you can prevent a negotiation degenerating into an argument and work instead towards a mutually satisfactory outcome. There is also some advice on preparing and giving a presentation, and taking part in a videoconference.

Should we have a meeting?

Not all meetings are necessary. You have probably attended quite a few where:

- nothing of any importance was decided
- there was no need for you to be there
- all you gained was some information which could just as easily have been put in the post

The only reason to hold a meeting is if it is the best way to communicate what has to be said. This is usually means that ideas are put forward and discussed – and decisions are taken. If people have no ideas or information to put forward, and no part in the decision-making process, there is no reason for them to be included in a meeting. Frequently, meetings are held to discuss matters which could be settled in a one-to-one discussion.

Many meetings are held out of habit. For example, it may be assumed that a department should meet every Monday, even if there is nothing to discuss. The agenda may be padded out with items which could be dealt with in other ways, to justify the existence of the meeting.

ACTIVITY 39

Think of two meetings you attended recently.

1 What percentage of the items discussed could have been dealt with in other ways?

Meeting 1:

Meeting 2:

2 What did you gain from attending the meetings?

Meeting 1:

Meeting 2:

3 What did your attendance at the meeting cost your organization, in terms of cash and your time?

Meeting 1:

Meeting 2:

FEEDBACK

If you add up the costs involved in bringing all the participants to a meeting, the figures can be alarming. Often the costs do not justify the benefits.

Most people do not work to their full capacity in a meeting. There is an interesting effect, described by the psychologist Adrian Furnham quoted at the start of this chapter, known as 'social loafing'. This phenomenon was first noticed by Ringleman, German scientist who compared the force that different-sized groups of people exerted on a rope.

- One person pulling a rope exerted an average force of 63 kilograms
- Three people in a group exerted an average force of 53 kilograms each
- Eight people in a group exerted an average force of 31 kilograms each

The more people who are in a group, the less effort each of them makes. You have probably observed this effect in large meetings.

Another problem with meetings is that they do not provide a particularly good forum for some people to speak. Some individuals may be intimidated by the presence of senior staff. Many people feel unwilling to put forward new ideas in a meeting, in case they are ridiculed or criticized. If you are trying to find a creative solution to a problem, a small, informal discussion may be much more productive.

To summarize, only hold a meeting if:

- something is going to happen as a result
- you can't come up with a better way to achieve this result

Preparing for a meeting

Once you are sure that you need a meeting, you must prepare for it properly. This involves:

- setting your objectives
- choosing the participants
- choosing your venue
- preparing your agenda

Objectives for meetings

You may have an overall objective for the meeting, or separate objectives for each item on the agenda. An objective should relate to the result which is to be achieved at the meeting.

ACTIVITY 40

Complete this sentence for a meeting held to decide which of four interview candidates is to be appointed:

By the end of this meeting we will ...

■ FEEDBACK

Compare your answer with this:

By the end of this meeting we will have reviewed the applications of the four interview candidates and come to a decision on whom we will appoint.

This is a SMART objective. It is:

- **S**imple enough for every one to understand
- **M**easurable – it will be easy to tell if it is has been achieved
- **A**chievable within a single meeting
- **R**ealistic – because it relates to what needs to be done
- **T**ime-related – because it will be done by the end of the meeting

Choosing the participants

The people you invite to a meeting will depend on what it is you are trying to achieve. If the meeting is being held to make a decision, then it is essential that those attending have the authority to make that decision – or have some useful input which will help the decision-making process. If it is sufficient for someone to be informed about the decision, he or she can be told about it afterwards.

Another common reason for holding a meeting is to motivate people. Here, it is essential that the people who need motivating are those who are present. This sounds obvious, but the right people are not always invited.

I went to a meeting about a new project. It included a wonderful presentation, and I went back to my department tremendously excited. But actually, I had been fully committed to the project before the meeting. It was my staff that needed convincing. I wish they had been able to see the presentation, too.

Everyone at a meeting should have a reason for being there.

ACTIVITY 41

Think back to the last meeting you attended. Who was there? What was the reason for each person's attendance?

Who: **Why:**

FEEDBACK

Was anybody there just to make the meeting look more impressive? Try not to make this mistake in meetings you organize yourself.

It is not always necessary for all the participants to be there for the entire meeting. If you organize your agenda along the lines we will describe in a moment, it should be possible to bring some people in for particular parts of the meeting.

Appoint someone who does not have another major role at the meeting to act as scribe. This individual should record important points and decisions, either privately or on a flip-chart, so that all participants can follow the progress that is being made. Do not try to act as scribe when you are chairing a meeting. The scribe's notes provide the basis for the minutes.

Choosing your venue

This choice will depend on:

- the size of your meeting
- the geographical location, and the importance, of your participants
- what people have to do in the meeting

If participants need to break up into smaller groups for part of the meeting, or watch a video, or look through a lot of papers during the meeting, make sure your choice of venue makes this possible.

Preparing your agenda

Most agendas list the topics that will be discussed. It is much more effective to write an objective-based agenda, like this:

> By the end of this meeting we will have:
>
> 1   Reviewed the results of the customer satisfaction survey and decided on any further action.
>
> 2   Decided how many hours of training consultancy time we need to include in next quarter's budget.
>
> 3   Decided which member of staff will receive this month's customer service award.

It is also useful if you can indicate how long each item of the agenda will take – and who will be involved in each item. You should also make sure that any papers that participants will need to refer to before the meeting go out with the agenda, and are referred to in the agenda itself.

A complete agenda could look like this:

Date: 16th July 1997
Place: Meeting room 7
Start: 10 am
Finish: 12 noon

Attendees: Chris Dunlop (chair), Philip Monroe (scribe), Ruth Badcock, Marsha Richards, Josh Liebemann.

By the end of this meeting we will have:

10–10.30 am
1   Reviewed the results of the customer satisfaction survey and decided on any further action. (See attached results summary.)
ALL
10.30–11.00 am
2   Decided how many hours of training consultancy time we need to include in next quarter's budget.
ALL
11.00–12 noon
3   Decided which member of staff will receive this month's customer service award. (See attached nominations papers.)
CD, DM, MR

ACTIVITY 42   D2.1, D3.1

Write an agenda in this format for a meeting you are planning to hold.

FEEDBACK

It takes slightly longer to prepare an agenda in this format, but the extra few minutes you spend on it should be repaid by the extra clarity and control you achieve in the meeting itself.

Chairing a meeting

The task of the chair is to ensure that the objectives of the meeting are met. If you have set out your objectives clearly in your agenda, this task will be easier to achieve.

Start a meeting on time, without waiting for latecomers. This is the best way to ensure that people arrive promptly the next time you ask them to a meeting. Only make exceptions to this rule if you risk causing offence to somebody important, such as a very senior manager or someone from a client organization. Welcome participants, review the agenda quickly and then move straight on to the first item.

When you open an agenda item, remind people of the objective and give any background information that may be necessary. If the participants at your meeting do not know each other, it may be helpful to point out who has particular knowledge or expertise in relation to the item under discussion. For example:

The first item is to decide who we send as a delegate to the conference on new packaging materials in Birmingham later this year. We always try to send someone along to this event so that they can produce a written report, keeping us up to speed in this area. I've asked Bill Parry from Despatch, who has attended the conference in the past but unfortunately can't go this year, to come along and answer any questions we may have about what's involved.

If you think that an item is likely to be contentious, it is useful to set some ground rules when you introduce it. For example:

Now, I know this is an area where feelings run high, so I'd like to keep the discussion as objective as possible. I'd be grateful if we could go round the table and hear what everybody has to say, without interruptions. Then we'll draw out the main issues which we've got to resolve.

Different types of agenda item have to be handled in different ways. If you have to make a decision, a useful structure to follow is:

- decide on the criteria
- examine the options in the light of these criteria
- make the decision

It helps if the scribe can record this process on a flip-chart.

If your objective is to review progress, you could follow this structure:

- identify what should have happened
- identify what has happened
- discuss the implications of any discrepancy between these two
- discuss difficulties ahead
- decide on further action

If it is important that you gain commitment to a decision from the meeting, make sure that you do this. Try to get everyone present to give their views. If some people do not speak, say that you are assuming that everyone goes along with the decision – and give them a final opportunity to come in. Before moving on to the next item on the agenda, summarize the main points and any decisions which have been made. If further action is to be taken, say who is doing what, and by when.

DEALING WITH DIFFICULT PEOPLE

The authors of *Successful Meetings in a Week* [2] identify six types of difficult people whom you may have to deal with at meetings:

- the perennial latecomer
- the talkative person
- the quiet (uninvolved) person
- the joker
- the person who blocks new ideas or change
- the aggressive person, who 'attacks' people

The perennial latecomer

Start the meeting without him or her. Don't stop and give a resumé the moment this person arrives, but let him or her wait and feel uncomfortable for a few minutes. As soon as you reach a point in the discussion where you can reasonably pause, introduce the latecomer (if necessary) and tell him or her what has happened so far.

The talkative person

Let this person have his or her fair say, as long as they stick to the point. Then summarize the key points he or she has made, thank them and immediately move the discussion on to someone else. It is difficult to interrupt someone who is determined to talk, but slightly easier if you use their name. For example:

'Jane, I wonder if I could stop you there ...'

If a talkative person keeps interrupting, remind them of the ground rules.

The quiet person

Some people say nothing, or very little, at a meeting. Quite frequently this is because they feel intimidated or out of their depth. You can encourage these people to contribute by asking them for their opinion. They are (or at least should be) present for a reason and it can help to boost their confidence if, at the start of the proceedings, you tell other participants what they have to offer to the meeting. For example:

> 'Malcolm has been running courses similar to the one we're considering today for several years.'

Some people say nothing because they profoundly disagree with what is being said, but feel that there is no point in voicing their opinions. This can be dangerous. If you don't bring these people into the discussion, they may not accept any decisions which are made. But if you do bring them in, you risk an argument. If you have participants like this, try to get them to articulate their opinions in a way which does not disrupt the meeting. Make sure that they assent to any decisions which are taken. If someone is very disenchanted with how things are going in the organization, this should probably be explored privately, outside the meeting.

The joker

Some humour is often welcome in a meeting. However, you may have a participant who does not know when to stop. In this case, say how you feel and ask for **relevant** suggestions.

The blocker

Some participants object to things without giving reasons. Don't ignore blockers. Instead, ask them to explain why they are objecting and then ask them to think of a solution. For example:

> A: 'I can't agree with that!'
> B: 'Why can't you agree?'
> A: 'Well, it's completely inappropriate.'
> B: 'In what way is it inappropriate?'
> A: 'The specifications are far too high.'
> B: 'What specifications do you think we should be asking for?'

The aggressor

The aggressive person makes personal attacks on other participants. It's important to step in quickly before the person who is attacked responds in a similar manner and you have an unpleasant and destructive argument on your hands. Tell the aggressor that personal attacks are unacceptable. For example:

'Wait a minute, Jerry. I can see that you don't agree with Martin, but it doesn't help to use that tone. Please keep to the issues here.'

If that doesn't work, call a coffee break to allow tempers to cool and have a quiet word with the aggressor.

AFTER A MEETING

Minutes must be written up from the scribe's notes and circulated. The minutes should relate to the objectives of the meeting. The amount of detail which is recorded can vary. Few people produce verbatim notes these days. It is more usual to record key points of the discussion and any decisions taken. The minutes should make it clear what further action was decided on, and who will take it, and by when.

Somebody should follow up progress after the meeting. It is important that this is done before the next meeting happens, or you may get a situation developing in which what is said and promised at meetings becomes strangely detached from reality.

Contributing to meetings

There are several things you can do as an ordinary participant to make a meeting go well. First of all, do your preparation. Read and reflect on any papers that are sent out with the agenda. Go through the agenda itself and, for each item, ask yourself the following questions:

- Do I have anything helpful to say?
- Is there anything I want to know?

Make notes on these points and bring them up at the meeting, if they are not raised by anyone else first.

ACTIVITY 43

Although you obviously would not categorize yourself as one of the 'difficult people' described earlier, have you ever:

- ❐ held other people up by arriving late?
- ❐ joined in a discussion when you had really nothing to add?
- ❐ not said what you felt until after the meeting?
- ❐ misjudged the tone of a discussion and made an inappropriate light-hearted remark?
- ❐ objected to proposals without explaining your reasons?
- ❐ let your annoyance with other participants show?

FEEDBACK

If you ticked any of these things, your behaviour at meetings may not have always been totally constructive.

Next, we will take a look at some communication skills which you may need in meetings where two opposing points of view have to be reconciled.

Negotiating

A negotiation is a specialized form of discussion in which the two (or more) parties have different objectives. There are three ways in which negotiations can end:

1 **win–lose**: one side gets what they want, but the other one doesn't
2 **lose–lose**: neither side gets what they want
3 **win–win**: both sides get enough of what they want to feel satisfied with the outcome

ACTIVITY 44

Imagine that you work for an organization in which the despatch of deliveries to customers is handled by an in-house department. Whenever you ask for an item to be sent out, a handling charge is deducted from your own department's budget. On occasions, the slowness of delivery to some customers has caused you severe embarrassment. You are trying to persuade the manager of the despatch department to provide a faster service.

Think about the following outcomes. Classify them as win–lose, lose–lose or win–win. How would you feel afterwards?

1   The manager of the despatch department refuses to budge. You accept the status quo.
    Type of outcome:
    How you would feel:

2   The manager of the despatch department refuses to budge. You write a strong memo to the managing director suggesting that you bring in an outside courier, at greater cost to your department, to send out your orders.
    Type of outcome:
    How you would feel:

3   You arrive at a compromise with the despatch department in which you will identify up to 10% of orders which should be given priority and for which you will pay a charge at a slightly higher rate. The rest of the orders will be treated in the normal way.
    Type of outcome:
    How you would feel:

4   Despite the manager's complaints that this will put a lot of strain on his staff, you persuade him to reduce the time it takes for all orders to be sent out and do not agree to an increase in charges.
    Type of outcome:
    How you would feel:

FEEDBACK

1   This is a win–lose result. When you lose and somebody else wins, you often feel frustrated, angry and resentful. Depending on the situation, your confidence may suffer. You may find it difficult to co-operate with the despatch department in future.

2   This is a lose–lose result. Neither side has got what they wanted. You may have involved yourself in extra expense and the despatch department may lose revenue. You probably feel frustrated, angry and resentful in this situation, too.

3   This is a win–win result. You have not achieved the objective you set out with, but you may feel quite happy with this result. You have established a new form of collaboration with the despatch department.

4   This is another win–lose result. This time you are on the winning side. You probably feel pleased about your victory. However, the manager of the despatch department is probably feeling as badly as you did under the first outcome. Relations between the two departments may be difficult in the future.

There are some occasions in business when achieving your objective is more important than the effect that decisions have on the people or organizations involved. However, most of the time, you will have to work with the people you are negotiating with again. If your victories have been gained at the expense of other individuals, you will build up a reservoir of resentment and distrust directed against you which will make future negotiations much more difficult. Therefore, whenever you can, you should try to achieve a win–win outcome to a negotiation.

PLANNING YOUR NEGOTIATIONS

In the first section of the book we discussed the importance of knowing your purpose when you are communicating. When you are entering negotiations, you have to be very specific about the outcome you are trying to achieve. You need to work out:

- your ideal outcome – the best you hope to achieve
- your realistic outcome – the result you could reasonably expect to achieve
- your fall-back position – the result you would be prepared to accept if you really had to

Also consider what would happen if negotiations broke down altogether. If you could live with this situation, your negotiating position would be much stronger. If you couldn't, then even achieving your fall-back position would mean that the negotiations had been a success.

You obviously do not reveal this analysis of the situation to the other side in the negotiations. You should, however, try to work out what their ideal, realistic and fall-back positions might be – and whether they can afford not to reach an agreement.

A fall-back position can be made more palatable if it is accompanied by extra benefits. These may not cost the other party much, but may add to the value of the package which is accepted.

The rules of bargaining can be summarized like this:

- Only give away things you can afford to lose.
- Only accept things that you want.
- Don't agree to anything you will regret later.
- Don't give anything away without getting something else in return

ACTIVITY 45

A friend is negotiating to buy a house. The property she is looking at has been on the market for a year. Your friend has got a firm buyer for her old house. The seller of the house she wants to buy is asking for £100,000. Your friend has made an offer of £90,000, although she could actually afford to pay the full asking price. The seller has refused to come down, but has offered to include all the carpets and curtains (which are not to your friend's taste) in the price. What would you advise your friend to do?

FEEDBACK

Your friend is in a very strong position. If negotiations break down, she can find another house. The seller is much less likely to find another buyer quickly. Your friend should not accept the carpets and curtains, which she doesn't want. From your friend's point of view, her ideal outcome is to buy at £90,000 and her fall-back position is to buy at £100,000. She should offer to split the difference and make an offer for £95,000. This is could be a realistic outcome for your friend, and may well be the seller's fall-back position.

ORGANIZING YOUR ARGUMENTS

When you are making a case, it is better to put forward one or two really good arguments than to offer a long list of reasons why a particular decision should be taken. If you put forward too many reasons, it is inevitable that some of these will not be as strong as others. And if the opposition can pick holes in any of your arguments, this will weaken your whole case.

Keep the other arguments in reserve. You may need to use them to answer objections that come up in the course of negotiations.

ACTIVITY 46

You are trying to persuade senior management to pay for an expensive piece of equipment for your department. Which of these arguments would you put forward to begin with, and which would you keep in reserve?

1   The equipment will result in efficiency savings and pay for itself in two years
2   You can get a discount of 10% if you order the equipment before the end of the month
3   Repair charges on your existing equipment are increasing each year
4   Your existing equipment presents a safety hazard and could contravene health and safety legislation
5   You have a member of staff who has had experience of using this equipment with another organization

FEEDBACK

Your best arguments in this situation are 1 and 4. Everything else can be kept in reserve and brought up to back up your case, if necessary.

When you prioritize your arguments, try to think about the situation from the point of view of the people you are trying to convince. In the activity you have just completed, senior management are likely to be most impressed by the promise of increased efficiency and profits and the need to keep within the law and to avoid endangering the safety of staff.

STATING YOUR POSITION

You cannot negotiate unless you can identify the areas where agreement has to be reached. It is important that both parties state their position as early in the negotiation as possible.

In the following example, manager A has started by outlining her proposal for a new training programme for her department to her boss, manager B.

> A: ....so, just to sum up, I'm proposing a series of half-day workshops to be provided by an outside trainer, which all staff would attend on a rotational basis six times a year. The costings I've prepared suggest that we could achieve this with a £5000 extension to our existing budget and I believe that the scheme would result in significant improvements to our turnaround time – and hence to our cash flow.
>
> B: It's a very attractive proposal. I can see the potential benefit to your cash flow, which would be extremely welcome. There are two problems which concern me, however. I am not sure we can make any budget changes within this financial period. And I'm rather worried at the disruption that might be caused by taking so many staff out of the office.

Now A knows the areas on which she may have to compromise:

■ the timing of the training programme – she may be able to get approval the following year
■ the involvement all staff – she may have to restrict the programme to certain key staff, or find a method of delivery which is not so disruptive to the work of her department

She also knows that B agrees with her about:

■ the need for the programme
■ the cost
■ the principle of involving outside trainers

This means that she does not have to bring in any further arguments to justify these points.

It is useful to all concerned if you can cover all the important issues on which you want agreement at the start of a negotiation. Some people only disclose their proposal in stages, usually because they are worried they have no chance of succeeding if they state all their demands at once.

> *A junior manager came and asked me if he could give a 15% discount on order to an established customer who was making a major investment in our products. I said yes, that's OK. Then he followed this up by asking if the customer could pay in 90 days on this occasion, rather than our usual 30 days. This annoyed me, because I felt manipulated. I said no, we couldn't do that, and the deal was off.*

It would have been better if this manager had disclosed both of the customer's requests at the start. Then there would at least have been room to manoeuvre.

At the beginning of a negotiation, state your ideal outcome. It will be more difficult to bring it in to the negotiations later on. Use your understanding of body language to judge how your initial proposal is received. Is the person you are negotiating with surprised, relaxed or perhaps particularly tense? Seasoned negotiators are good at disguising their reactions, however, and you may not get all the feedback you want. One way to find out their position is to ask an open question.

'How does that match up with your ideas on the situation?'
'What suggestions would you like to make?'
'What figure did you have in mind?'
'You seem a little uncertain about that last point. Why is that?'

ACTIVITY 47

You will need a friend or colleague to help you with this activity. Don't use this exercise to discuss anything about which either you or the other person feels strongly.

1 Put a proposal to the other person about changing some existing arrangement
2 Put forward your best arguments and state your ideal outcome
3 Use your questioning skills and your understanding of body language to discover their reaction
4 Summarize the areas where you have agreement and disagreement

FEEDBACK

Don't expect to get instant agreement at the start of a negotiation. Your aim at this stage should be to explain as clearly as possible what you would like to happen and to gauge the other side's reaction and/or hear their counterproposals. This will tell you the issues on which you will have to work to find an agreement.

KEEPING CONTROL OF THE DISCUSSION

It is often helpful in negotiations to signal what stage has been reached:

> 'I've outlined what I see as the advantages of the scheme. I'd be interested in hearing your first reactions.'
> 'OK, we're both happy about the delivery date. Let's think about the price next.'
> 'We've agreed that we want to take this idea on to the next stage. We can't go any further with the specification until Desmond gets back on Friday. Let's now think about the safety criteria we should set.'

Signals like this help structure the discussion and remind people of the things they have agreed to.

If you find the negotiation is wandering off the point, you can use chunking up to bring it back on line. For example:

> 'I can see that there are a number of details which will need resolving, but I'm interested to know your feelings about the general principle of relocation.'

Keeping the temperature down

If negotiations become heated, this makes it much more difficult to reach agreement. If you are confronted by someone who is getting angry, a useful technique is to separate facts from opinions. If you refuse to react to opinions, but concentrate on seeking and providing facts, the emotional level of the conversation can be brought back to normal. Once this has happened, the issue which has provoked the outburst may be resolved surprisingly easily.

Defence and attack

If you attack somebody in a negotiation, he or she will probably react defensively and may well come back at you with a counterattack. If you then defend yourself, the discussion is well on the way to becoming a full scale argument.

When you disagree with somebody, argue about the issues and leave personalities out of it. Remember, your aim is to persuade that individual to move from the position he or she is occupying. If you make your opponent feel personally under attack, he or she will defend the position to the death.

If you are verbally attacked, try to ignore any personal indignation you may feel and concentrate on the issues. It is hard to continue attacking somebody who refuses to fight back. Look at how manager A reacts in these two versions of the same dialogue.

Version 1

> A: I'd be grateful if you could let me have your revised figures by Friday morning.
>
> B: I'm sorry, but that's an outrageous request. I do have a department to run.
>
> A: And I've got a budget to get ready for the Managing Director on Monday morning.
>
> B: You should have thought about that when you asked me for the figures.
>
> A: If you'd been any good at your job you'd have read my memo properly and produced the figures in the form I asked for.

Version 2

> A: I'd be grateful if you could let me have your revised figures by Friday morning.
>
> B: I'm sorry, but that's an outrageous request. I have a department to run.
>
> A: How many hours do you estimate you'll need to revise your figures?
>
> B: Three or four hours minimum. But I've got meetings back to back all week.
>
> A: Are there any of these meetings you could reschedule between now and Friday?
>
> B: Well, I suppose I don't actually have to attend the Brighton conference all day on Wednesday. I could go through the figures on Wednesday morning.

Manager A gets the agreement he needs here by refusing to enter into a spiral of defence and attack. Instead, he focuses on finding a way in which the problem can be solved.

Finding a creative solution

If you ever reach deadlock in a negotiation, you may need to step back from the situation and look at it from a different angle. It is possible that there is another route that you can take to achieve your objectives.

For example, suppose that you are negotiating to buy a specialized piece of equipment which is only available from a single supplier. You cannot pay more than £5000 because this is all you have in your annual budget. The supplier refuses to drop the price below £6000. If they go any lower, they will not be covering their overheads. You have reached deadlock.

ACTIVITY 48

Can you see any common ground between the two parties in this situation?

FEEDBACK

The thing that both parties have in common is that they would like the sale to go through, albeit on different terms.

Once you have established the common ground, the parties may be able to help each other to find a solution. Here, it might be possible for the suppliers to accept a downpayment of, say, £4000, with the remaining £2000 in your next budget period. Or the supplier might be able to provide you with an ex-demonstration model at a lower price. Or you might be able to reduce the supplier's overheads by collecting the equipment yourself. You may be able to think of other potential solutions. The trick is to transform a negotiation from an adversarial contest into a creative search for a mutually acceptable solution – a win–win outcome.

ACTIVITY 49   D2.2, D3.2

Conclude your work in this section by analysing a negotiation in which you are involved at work. You may learn most from this activity if you choose a negotiation in which you have a fairly minor role. Listen and watch for the communication skills which both parties use in this situation.

1   As soon as possible afterwards, make notes on:
    - what both parties wanted to achieve from the negotiation
    - the outcome
    - communication skills which helped towards a satisfactory outcome to the negotiation
    - communication skills which made it more difficult to arrive at a satisfactory outcome
2   Then make two lists about your own communication skills:
    - techniques which you will try to avoid in future
    - new communication techniques which you would like to use in future

FEEDBACK
You cannot learn to be a skilled negotiator overnight. However, by intelligent observation of successful (and unsuccessful) techniques used by other people, you can develop your own skills. Your work in this section should have highlighted some important principles of negotiation which you can explore in more depth in your working environment.

Presentations

A presentation is any talk which is given to a group. It can be a briefing which you give to your team, or a major speech delivered to an invited audience. Whatever the scale of your presentation, the same principles apply.

PREPARING A PRESENTATION

If you are invited to give a presentation, decide whether you should accept. If you don't have the time to prepare properly, or somebody else would do a better job than you, then decline the invitation. If you accept, find out as many details as you can about what is expected of you.

ACTIVITY 50

Imagine that you have been invited to give a presentation at a conference. What details do you need to know? Use the journalist's questions to compile a list of queries for the conference organizer.

- Who?
- What?
- Why?
- Where?
- When?
- How?

FEEDBACK

You would need to know:

- Who is your audience? Who else will be speaking?
- What exactly will you be speaking about?
- Why are you giving the presentation – what is your purpose?
- Where will you be giving it?
- When are you giving it? When will you be able to prepare the room?
- How will you give your presentation? What facilities are available?

Think about your audience. What do they know already and what do they need to know? Also consider whether your main purpose will be to inspire, to persuade, to inform or to entertain.

Next, prepare your material. You can use the techniques suggested in the section on writing to help you here. You have already encountered the best structure for a presentation:

- position
- problem
- possibilities
- proposal

Begin by talking about the present situation in a way that means something to your audience. This will draw them into what you have to say. Then introduce your problem – the complication which means that things cannot go on as they are. Then discuss possible ways forward and put forward your proposal as the best solution to the problem. This is the core structure of your presentation. You must also preface it with a few remarks to put your audience at their ease, and end with a postcript.

- preface
- position
- problem
- possibilities
- proposal
- postscript

ACTIVITY 51

Make some notes to show how you could use this structure to plan a talk you are giving to your own department about a change in working arrangements.

FEEDBACK

If you could use this structure in a situation in which you are fairly comfortable, now try using it to plan a more ambitious presentation.

Once you have planned the outline of your presentation, write your script. Draft it and then edit it, simplifying your style. Read your script out to a friend or colleague and ask him or her to take notes and give you feedback afterwards. Vary the texture of your presentation, so that you keep your audience's interest. Most people's attention will decrease after the first ten minutes, and then increase as the end of the presentation approaches. You will have to work harder to keep your audience's attention in the intervening period.

Pick out key words and phrases from your script and write these prompts on cards. Practise giving your presentation from these cards alone. Don't try to memorize and repeat every word of your original, just use the prompt cards to keep you on track. If your presentation is very formal, or copies of your speech have been handed out to the press, you will have to read from your original script. In other circumstances, however, use cards.

Choose what visual aids you will use to illustrate your presentation. These might include:

- **Prepared flip-charts**   These are effective, and are not used as frequently as they could be. Keep them bold and simple
- **Flip-charts**   These can be useful if you are involving your audience in your presentation. You can pencil in guidelines to help you draw diagrams during the presentation – your audience won't be able to see them
- **Overhead Projector (OHP)**   Transparencies are a very popular visual aid. Keep them as simple as possible. Never put more words on a slide than you would on a T shirt!
- **35mm slides**   These can be effective, but you will be very dependent on the equipment working properly. You may also lose the audience's attention if you have to keep turning the lights out
- **Videos**   Videos are impressive, but may not be completely appropriate to your subject or audience if they have not been made specially for the occasion, which is probably prohibitively expensive. They can also break the flow of your presentation

If you are speaking to fewer than ten people, you may only need simple visual aids. You should aim for an informal style with a small audience like this. For an audience of ten to thirty people, you will need to speak more formally and should definitely use visual aids. For a larger audience still, you should use the most professional-looking aids.

Decide at what point in your presentation you will use your visual aids, for maximum effect. Once you have prepared your visuals, rehearse your presentation with these elements in place.

GIVING A PRESENTATION

When you arrive at the venue, check:

- your equipment
- your visual aids
- your appearance

Allow as much time as you can, so you can be sure that any problems are sorted out before the presentation begins.

When you stand up to speak, take a moment to establish your presence with the audience. Take a deep breath and look at the people you are talking to. Make eye contact with them. Try to relax, and smile.

If your audience doesn't know you, you must start by explaining who you are and what you will be speaking about. Also tell them what gives you the authority to be giving the presentation. Give your audience an idea of how long the presentation will last, and whether there will be any breaks. Tell them whether you want people to interrupt if they have a question, or wait until the end of the session. Once your audience knows what to expect, they will start to relax, and this will help you to relax, too.

Your next task is to involve your audience in what you are saying. An interesting or surprising visual aid can help here, or an unexpected remark or a rhetorical question. Once you have got their attention, you can draw them into your argument.

Dealing with problems in a presentation

The thing that most speakers dread happening in a presentation is stage fright. If you are familiar and comfortable with the material you are presenting, this is much less likely to happen. You can also help yourself to feel relaxed by establishing eye contact with your audience. If you do feel yourself tensing up, make an effort to speak more slowly. Speak naturally, but lower the pitch of your voice. Use positive body language. Stand erect, and don't fiddle with your hair or clothing. Basically, try to **act** as if you feel relaxed. Your nerves will probably pass quickly. If you do dry up, just pause for a moment, and then carry on.

Equipment failure is another potential problem. Check everything that could possibly go wrong before you begin. If something unexpected does happen, don't let it throw you. Your audience will be more impressed by how you handle the situation than by the disaster itself.

Difficult questions from the audience can put you off balance. Try to anticipate the worst questions you could be asked, and prepare your answers. If you are asked a question you cannot answer, don't try to bluff your way out. It is much simpler, and will command more respect, if you admit ignorance and, depending on the circumstances, deal with the question by referring to an expert colleague, promising to find out the answer later, or opening it up to the audience.

ACTIVITY 52   D4.4

The next time you attend a presentation, make notes on how it was delivered. Make lists of:

■ things which went well
■ things which could have gone better

Did you see any techniques which you could incorporate into your own presentations?

FEEDBACK

Use every presentation you attend as an opportunity to learn more about the techniques involved and add to your own repertoire of skills.

We will end this section by looking at a form of meeting which makes use of the latest technology.

Videoconferencing

UK companies spend over £1 billion on business travel in a year. Videoconferencing, which uses ISDN lines to transmit audio and video signals between different sites, can make some of this travel unnecessary and, most importantly, enable quick decisions.

Videoconferencing systems are relatively expensive. Not surprisingly, the more you pay, the better the quality of the sound and pictures that are transmitted. With a six line system (340 kbts), the picture approaches the definition you would expect from an ordinary television. The equipment can be installed in an office with an ISDN connection. Alternatively, you can hire the facilities at a local videoconferencing centre.

Many videoconferences are between two sites but multipoint conferences are possible. The two main types of multipoint system currently in use are:

- continuous presence, in which the screen is split up and everyone is on camera all the time
- voice operated, in which the person who is speaking is automatically shown on screen

CASE STUDY

Here is some advice from the Octagon in Docklands, a conference centre which runs a videoconferencing bureau:

'We tell clients that videoconferencing can't replace face-to-face meetings altogether. There's some extra ambience when you're actually in the same room as someone else which you can't capture on camera. That said, videoconferencing is an excellent way to keep contacts going between people who have already met, or who are going to meet in the future.

'Multipoint conferencing makes it possible to link many sites. Five sites is a practical number – the maximum that it is sensible to use. In every room, you can have several people – six is a sensible number.

'Like any meeting, a videoconference needs discipline. If everyone talks at once, nobody can hear what is said. This is particularly important if you are using a voice-operated system.

'You need a chairperson to control the discussion. Basically, you run a videoconference like a normal meeting. Everyone greets each other, then the chairperson calls the meeting to order, introduces the participants and starts on the agenda. There are a few extra points to be aware of, however:

- **Lighting**   Don't have strong lighting from above, or people will have long shadows under their noses. Don't make people face straight into a bright light, either.
- **Movement**   If people move around a lot, they may go out of shot. Hand movements can be distracting, so we remind people to keep their hands in front of them, or resting on the table. Even with the latest technology, rapid movements can cause a 'ghosting' effect on the screen.
- **Camera**   Some systems use a camera which can zoom in and out, or pan from one side of the room to the other. In this case, you need someone whose main job in the meeting is to operate the camera. Don't expect the chairperson to do it at the same time as controlling the meeting. The camera operator should be next to the chairperson.'

Some systems allow you to bring more elements into your videoconference. For example, you can:

- use an electronic camera to give high resolution pictures of objects you want to examine
- use a visualizer (an OHP with a video camera)
- transmit documents
- link up with a multimedia program to introduce still pictures, videos and recorded sound
- use a roving microphone to bring members of an audience into a discussion

The technology in this area is developing rapidly. Videoconferencing is likely to become a much more common part of business life.

ACTIVITY 53

Look through your diary and think about the meetings you have planned for the next month. Could any of these be replaced by a videoconference?

FEEDBACK

If you haven't used videoconferencing yet, why not find out what facilities you and the other participants have available locally? Your local bureau can find distant sites for you.

Summary

Now that you have finished this section you should be able to:

- decide whether you really need a meeting
- decide the objectives for a meeting
- invite appropriate participants to a meeting
- prepare an agenda
- chair a meeting
- deal with difficult people at a meeting
- contribute positively to a meeting
- prioritize your arguments in a negotiation

- state your opening position in a negotiation
- keep a negotiation on course towards a successful conclusion
- plan and deliver an effective presentation
- set up and take part in a videoconference

Notes

1 Furnham, A. (1996) *All In the Mind*, Whurr Publishers Ltd
2 Payne, J. and Payne, S. (1994) *Successful Meetings In a Week*, Headway, Hodder & Stoughton/The Institute of Management Foundation

Summary

Now that you have finished this book, you should be able to:

- give appropriate consideration to why, what, when, and how you are communicating
- take account of the needs of your audience
- use verbal and non-verbal techniques for active listening
- ask effective questions
- use the telephone effectively
- plan the contents of what you write
- use an appropriate structure for your writing
- write effective letters, proposals and reports
- use e-mail effectively
- use a clear and concise writing style
- calculate the readability of your writing
- present your writing effectively
- use a range of reading skills in appropriate situations
- plan, set up and control meetings effectively
- contribute positively to a meeting
- use negotiation skills
- plan and deliver an effective presentation
- set up and take part in a videoconference

Recommended reading

Further reading

Bird, P. (1994) *Tame That Phone: Controlling the tyranny of the telephone*, Pitman Publishing/The Institute of Management Foundation

Cochrane, P. (1994) *The Power of the Phone: Tested Techniques to Cut Costs, Save Time and Boost Sales*, Pitman Publishing/The Institute of Management Foundation

Jay, A. (1993) *Effective Presentation*, Pitman Publishing/The Institute of Management Foundation

Jay, R. (1994) *How to Write Proposals and Reports that Get Results* Pitman Publishing/The Institute of Management Foundation

Martin, D. M. (1993) *Tough Talking: How to Handle Awkward Situations*, Pitman Publishing/The Institute of Management Foundation

Martin, D. M. (1994) *Manipulating Meetings: How to Get What You Want, When You Want It*, Pitman Publishing/The Institute of Management Foundation

Martin, D. M. (1995) *How To Be a Great Communicator: The Complete Guide to Mastering Internal Communication*, Pitman Publishing/The Institute of Management Foundation

Michelli, D. (1994) *Successful Assertiveness In a Week*, Headway, Hodder & Stoughton/The Institute of Management Foundation

Payne, J. and Payne, S. (1994) *Successful Meetings In a Week*, Headway, Hodder & Stoughton/The Institute of Management Foundation

Peel, M. (1995) *Successful Presentation In a Week*, Headway, Hodder & Stoughton/The Institute of Management Foundation

Wainwright, G. W. (1993) *Successful Business Writing In a Week*, Headway, Hodder & Stoughton/The Institute of Management Foundation

Wainwright, G. W. (1993) *Tricky Business Letters: Persuasive Tactics on Paper*, Pitman Publishing/The Institute of Management Foundation

Checklist 002 Handling effective meetings

Checklist 018 Planning a workshop

Checklist 031 Effective communications: delivering presentations

Checklist 032 Effective communications: planning presentations

Checklist 039 Planning a conference

Checklist 051 Report writing

Checklist 080 Designing questionnaires

The Institute of Management Foundation

About the Institute of Management

The mission of the Institute of Management (IM) is to promote the development, exercise and recognition of professional management.

The IM is the leading professional organization for managers. Its efforts and resources are devoted to ensuring the continuing development and success of its members.

At the forefront of management standards, the IM provides a range of services for its members. These include flexible training programmes and a unique range of support services such as career counselling, enquiry and research facilities and preferential prices on IM publications and other IM products.

Further details about the Institute of Management may be obtained from:

Institute of Management
Management House
Cottingham Road
Corby
Northants
NN17 1TT

Telephone 01536 204222

We need your views

We really need your views in order to make the Institute of Management Open Learning Programme an even better learning tool for you. Please take time out to complete and return this questionnaire to Marketing Department, Flexible Learning, Linacre House, Jordan Hill, Oxford OX2 8DP

Name:...

Address:...

....

Title of workbook:..

If applicable, please state which qualification you are studying for. If not, please describe what study you are undertaking, and with which organization or college:

....

Please grade the following out of 10 (10 being extremely good, 0 being extremely poor):

Content: ....   Suitability for ability level: ....

Readability: ....   Qualification coverage: ....

What did you particularly like about this workbook?

....

Are there any features you disliked about this workbook? Please identify them.

....

Are there any errors we have missed?
If so, please state page number: ....

How are you using the material? For example, as an open learning course, as a reference resource, as a training resource, etc.

....

How did you hear about the Institue of Management Open Learning Programme?:

Word of mouth: Through my tutor/trainer: Mailshot:

Other (please give details):...

Many thanks for your help in returning this form.

Institute of Management Open Learning Programme

This programme comprises seventeen workbooks, each on a core management topic with the latest management thinking, as well as a *User Guide* and a *Mentor Guide*.

Designed for self study through open learning, the workbooks cover all management experience from team building to budgeting, from the skills of self management to manage strategically for organizational success.

TITLE	ISBN	Price
The Influential Manager	0 7506 3662 9	£22.50
Managing Yourself	0 7506 3661 0	£22.50
Getting the Right People to Do the Right Job	0 7506 3660 2	£22.50
Understanding Business Process Management	0 7506 3659 9	£22.50
Customer Focus	0 7506 3663 7	£22.50
Getting TQM to Work	0 7506 3664 5	£22.50
Leading from the Front	0 7506 3665 3	£22.50
Improving Your Organization's Success	0 7506 3666 1	£22.50
Project Management	0 7506 3667 X	£22.50
Budgeting and Financial Control	0 7506 3668 8	£22.50
Effective Financial and Resource Management	0 7506 3669 6	£22.50
Developing Yourself and Your Staff	0 7506 3670 X	£22.50
Building a High Performance Team	0 7506 3671 8	£22.50
The New Model Leader	0 7506 3672 6	£22.50
Making Rational Decisions	0 7506 3673 4	£22.50
Communication	0 7506 3674 2	£22.50
Successful Information Management	0 7506 3675 0	£22.50
User Guide	0 7506 3676 9	£22.50
Mentor Guide	0 7506 3677 7	£22.50
Full set of workbooks plus *Mentor Guide* and *User Guide*	0 7506 3359 X	£370.00

To order: *(Please quote ISBNs when ordering)*

- College Orders: 01865 314333
- Account holders: 01865 314301
- Individual Purchases: 01865 314627

  (Please have credit card details ready)

  For further information or to request a full series brochure, please contact:

  Tessa Gingell on 01865 314477